TOUCHED
BY A
Miracle

Other books by Nathalie Ladner-Bischoff

An Angel's Touch

TOUCHED
BY A
Miracle

More true stories about angels, miracles,

and answers to prayer

Author of *An Angel's Touch*

Nathalie Ladner-Bischoff

PACIFIC PRESS® PUBLISHING ASSOCIATION
Nampa, Idaho
Oshawa, Ontario, Canada
www.PacificPress.com

Designed by Michelle C. Petz
Cover photo © Sean Justice / Getty Images

Copyright © 2004 by
Pacific Press® Publishing Association
Printed in the United States of America
All Rights Reserved

Additional copies of this book are available by calling toll free 1-800-765-6955
or by visiting www.AdventistBookCenter.com

Library of Congress Cataloging-in-Publication Data

Ladner-Bischoff, Nathalie, 1931-
Touched by a miracle : more true stories about angels, miracles,
and answers to prayer / Nathalie Ladner-Bischoff.
p. cm.
ISBN 0-8163-2010-1

BT966.3.L33 2004
235'.3—dc22   2003066417

04 05 06 07 08 · 5 4 3 2

Dedication

With gratitude to each of those who contributed stories to this book—especially Mabel Latsha and Helen Bishop for their unfailing encouragement and their willingness to share so many instances of God's amazing ways.

Contents

CHAPTER I

My Handsome Comforter

February 28, 2001, began as any other day. I awoke at 6:30 A.M., showered, dressed, and got ready for work. At 7:20 I left my apartment and drove to the park, where I caught the shuttle bus that transported me to downtown Seattle. A few minutes before 8:00 I arrived at my desk on the thirty-second floor of the building where I worked as a discount broker for an investment firm.

Around 9:40 A.M. I was talking to a client on the phone when my computer monitor bounced slightly on my desk! My first thought was that a co-worker was playing a trick on me. I peeked around the corner of my cubicle, but saw no one. Then I turned and looked at the person sitting in the cubicle diagonally across from me. We locked eyes for a second, and then she shouted, "We're having an earthquake! Get under your desk!" I quickly told my client I had to leave, hung up the phone, and scrambled under my desk.

I could feel the floor shaking and my computer thumping violently up and down on my desk. The skyscraper swayed sickeningly. I never knew tall buildings were built to move like that! I had joked from time to time with other workers about what it would be like on the thirty-second floor when "the big one" hit. But this was no joke! This was terrifying reality! Thoughts of dying raced through my mind. I panicked! Crying and trembling, I pictured the skyscraper breaking in half; I could see myself tumbling thirty-two stories to a certain death!

Suddenly, a young man appeared at my cubicle. "Are you all right?" he asked.

Hysterical and unable to speak, I just shook my head.

He crawled under the desk beside me, put his arm around my shoulders, and said, "It will be over soon!" Just having him there with me underneath the trembling desk calmed me. He was a young, handsome, Hispanic man dressed in grey slacks and a matching shirt. I had never seen him on my floor before—and I knew everyone on my floor.

After the longest minutes of my life, the building quit shaking. The young man and I crawled from under my desk. Dazed and in shock, I stood and watched my co-workers emerging from under their desks. People started asking each other, "Are you OK?"

I turned to thank the young man who had gotten under my desk to calm me. He was nowhere in sight! I looked all around me, but he had vanished! *It's odd,* I thought, *that he had been walking around in the middle of an earthquake.*

"Do either of you know who that young man was who crawled under my desk with me during the quake?" I asked two co-workers standing nearby.

They looked puzzled. "We didn't see anyone under your desk with you," they said. One added, "Tosha, it must have been your guardian angel!"

For three more months after the earthquake, I continued working for the investment firm on the thirty-second floor. Not a day passed that terror didn't grip me each time I entered the building. Every time someone walked by my cubicle and I felt the vibrations in the floor and in my desk, my heart raced. I often looked for the young man who'd climbed under the desk with me to give me comfort and assurance during the quake, but I never saw him again.

When I told my grandmother what had happened, she said, "I believe that was your guardian angel, honey! Every day I pray that God will protect you, and I'm sure God sent His angel to protect you in answer to my prayers!"

I'm still not sure that God sent an angel to look after me. But I have to believe that if that young man *was* an angel, he was there for a good reason. I'll always be grateful for the comfort he gave me that day. I wish I could thank him personally. And maybe someday, I will!

As told by Tosha Knopp.

CHAPTER 2

Amazed by His Ways

On New Year's Day, 1995, I went skiing at Anthony Lakes with my two sons. After we finished lunch, I went to the car to call Ruby, my wife, on my mobile phone. I just wanted to tell her about the good time we were having. After talking to Ruby, I locked the phone back in the car and put the keys in my pocket. The weather was beautiful, and we were having a great time. We had gone up the hill on the ski lift twice when Jeff asked me to get his camera from the car. At the car, I reached in my pocket for the keys—and discovered they had disappeared! Evidently, I had forgotten to zip shut the pocket when I had put the keys in my parka earlier.

I panicked.

Somewhere on that mountain are my car keys, I thought, looking at the huge mountain of white. *They're hopelessly buried in the snow on some slope. Now what are we going to do? How in the world will we get back home?*

I would have to call Ruby and ask her to bring us the extra

keys to the car. That meant she would have to drive two hours to Anthony Lakes.

"Have you prayed?" Jeff asked.

The words were like a slap in my face. I am a pastor. I've tried to fortify other people's faith in trying situations. Now it was my turn. It seems I heard the Lord whisper, "Oh you of little faith!" Then a comforting thought came to my mind. *God knows where those keys are. He could lead us to them.* So I prayed, "Lord, You know where the keys are on this big mountain. Please help us find them."

Before I called Ruby, Mike and I decided to take the chairlift to the top of the mountain. We would visually scour the hillside. *But if the keys had fallen from my pocket while I was on the chairlift,* I told myself, *they would have buried themselves deep in the snow.*

When we got to the top, I tried to think where the keys would have most likely fallen from my pocket. It would have been on Star Bottle Run, the slope of moguls, I decided.

Telling Mike to take the right side, I took the left. We started down, slowly side-slipping as we went. I was halfway down the slope. My faith was still very weak, and I was ready to give up. The key ring had a black door button and a Singapore bug inlaid in plastic, which would make it easy to identify. I stopped and turned to look up toward Mike. He was moving slowly. Then he stopped, pointing. "There they are!" he shouted. Lying there on the snow was that little bug from Singapore!

My doubts suddenly turned to joy and praise. I could hardly believe my eyes as Mike reached down and picked up the keys. All I could say was, "Praise the Lord! This is a miracle!"

My faith is stronger now that I have personally experienced the fact that God is able to do all things—even find a set of lost keys on the snowy slopes of a ski run. The experience also taught me to keep my keys zipped shut inside my pocket the next time I go skiing!

I've learned, too, that if losing my keys caused me so much concern, how much more so I should be when souls are lost. God is also able to find them, and I must cooperate with Him by looking for them and bringing them to Him.

Written by John Stafford.
First published in He's Alive, *Volume 11, Numbers 3, 4.*
Used by permission.

CHAPTER 3

My Guardian Angel

For years I've had a regular Friday morning appointment at a certain beauty shop on Second Street. I don't feel ready for Sabbath unless I have my hair shampooed, set, and styled every Friday. One Thursday night in December it rained, then froze, and finally snowed four inches on top of the ice. Friday morning I looked out of my window and saw treacherous streets. I didn't know what to do about my hair appointment. *Should I cancel? Or should I bravely venture out on the ice and snow?* I wondered. I pondered the decision for some time.

I'd had a total hip replacement a few months earlier, so I didn't feel steady on my feet—especially on snow and ice. But my cane gave me a sense of security, and I decided to keep my appointment. I would take my cane and walk very cautiously from my car to the beauty shop.

There were no problems as I drove to Second Street. And I was fortunate to find a parking spot very near to the beauty shop door. But I still needed to negotiate the ice and snow between my car door and the cleared, dry sidewalk. I reached for my cane. It wasn't in its usual place beside me! I'd forgotten my cane; I'd left it at home.

What shall I do now? I questioned. *Go home and get my cane?* I'd be late for my appointment. And I'd likely lose my good parking spot. I decided I could manage the short distance from my car to the sidewalk without the cane.

Slowly and carefully I got out of the car. Hanging on to the door for a moment, I stood on the snow and prayed, "Dear God, please keep me from falling as I carefully venture toward the sidewalk!" I closed the car door and steadied myself. Holding to the car, I inched my way slowly past the rear door to the back of the vehicle. I paused, hoping someone would come along that I could ask to help me to the sidewalk. I looked up the street, then down the street. I looked every direction, but there wasn't a soul in sight—not even a cat, dog, or squirrel. Nothing! I hesitated to let go of the car and walk alone on the snow. Again I looked around me. I could see for blocks in every direction. Nothing was moving; there was no one in sight who could help me. For an instant I just stood there praying for help.

Then I heard a voice say, "It's pretty icy this morning, isn't it?"

I glanced up and saw a pleasant looking Black man standing on the sidewalk nearby. He wore a cap on his head, but he wasn't wearing a coat even though the temperature hovered around twenty degrees Fahrenheit.

"Oh sir, am I glad to see you! Could you please help me?" I asked. "I'm so afraid of falling on this ice!"

"Sure, I'd be happy to help you!" he said. He strolled toward me across the ice and snow as if it weren't there. As he drew near, he held out his hand, and I took it. With my arm locked in his, I had all the support I needed. He easily took me the several steps to the cleared sidewalk.

Once safely there, I said, "Thank you, sir. I can make it on my own now. You'll never know how much I appreciate your help!"

"Are you sure you can make it on your own?" he asked. "I'd be very happy to take you to the door."

"Thank you. You have been most kind, and I really do appreciate your help. But I can manage now."

"No problem!" he replied.

I took just one step and turned to look at him once more—but there was no one in sight! In that instant, he had disappeared. I looked in every direction. No one. The man was gone!

I know God answered my prayer, and I'm grateful to Him for sending an angel to help me walk safely across the ice and snow. If I'd known it was an angel, I would have held on to his arm a little longer and allowed him to escort me to the door!

I told the ladies in the beauty shop about my experience, but none of them made a comment. As the beautician gave my hair the final touches, she said, "Let's get our coats on. I'll walk you out to your car." She realized I was worried about returning to the car on my own. The Lord impressed her to be my second "angel."

This encounter with an angel did something for me that I cannot fully explain. It has strengthened my faith in God's caring and protecting power. I know for sure that He knows our every need even before we call on Him—and He holds the answer! I thank Him for my guardian angel who came to my aid that icy December morning!

As told by Edna Wagner.

CHAPTER 4

Kern River Rescue

Among the people who have influenced my life, one stands out even though my encounter with him lasted only five minutes or so. I met him thirty years ago, when our family was camping by the Kern River in California.

We pitched our tent on a beautiful sand bar beside a quiet stretch of the river. My brother, Rick, twelve, and I, ten, kicked and paddled around on our inner tubes in the calm water. What fun we had splashing, squealing, and chasing each other! I didn't swim well, so I was totally dependent on my inner tube to keep me afloat.

One day Dad suggested, "Why don't you boys float down the river to the park that is about a mile away. Mom and I will meet you at the bridge there."

So Rick and I headed down the river. At first, all went well. Soon, however, the calm water ended, and we faced a churning torrent. My father hadn't seen these rapids; he didn't know how treacherous the river quickly became below our camp. Shaking with fright, I wanted to stop, but Rick raced forward toward the white water.

"Stop, Rick! I can't go! We've got to pray first." Our family had just started going to church, and I had recently learned to pray. So trembling, I said with quivering lips, "Please, God, watch over us as we shove into this rough water." I knew once we headed into the turbulence, there was no return.

Rick went first. Petrified, I stood and watched a tumbling current swiftly carry him fifty or sixty feet ahead of me. Then, trying to stay near the edge of the forty-foot-wide river, I slowly paddled into the raging water. A swirling current swept me into the churning foam. Ahead, I saw my brother disappear over a three-foot water fall. Clutching his inner tube, he bounced like a cork at the base of the fall. The seething water seemed to hold him captive, spinning him around and around and bobbing him up and down. Eventually, he floated into a gushing stream of water that threw him free of the falls.

Breathless, I clung to my inner tube and thought, *No way am I going down that water fall!* With all my might, I fought, kicked, and paddled toward the river's edge. But as I neared the shore, the current pulled me around a big rock. On the far side lay an old piano. The current bounced me against it, and a nail protruding from the piano ripped a hole as big as my fist in my tube. Then the wild water kicked me back into the middle of the river with nothing to hang on to but my deflated tube! As the rushing current pushed me down river, I panicked and screamed. About seventy-five feet ahead of me, Rick looked back, and laboriously pushed toward shore. Just then I saw a fisherman standing in the water. As I tumbled passed him, he reached out, grabbed me, and pulled me to shore.

"Where are your parents?" he asked.

Shivering like a leaf, I pointed down the river. "They're waiting for us at the bridge." He started walking toward the bridge with Rick and me, but I said, "We can make it from here."

When we got to the bridge and told our parents what had happened, Dad said, "Let's go back and thank that fisherman for saving your life." We walked back together, but couldn't find the fisherman anywhere.

Last year I returned to our camping spot of years ago. The banks of the Kern are overgrown with weeds now, but I was able walk down the river and find the rapids from which the fisherman saved me. Sitting on a rock, I watched the raging river. Excited people screamed as their rafts tumbled past. Right there by the river, I got down on my knees and thanked God for sparing my life that long-ago day when I was ten.

I've always wondered about the fisherman who pulled me out of the river. As I bedded down in my camper the night of my return, I prayed, "Dear God, I'd really like to know if that fisherman was an angel. I believe he was. Please give me some clarity on this."

I awoke the next morning disappointed. I had thought that perhaps God would have me relive the experience in a dream and reveal to me that the fisherman was an angel. But nothing like that happened.

That morning, however, when I opened my Bible, it fell open to a place where someone had inserted a picture. Psalm 91 was marked on the page. I read the whole Psalm. Verses 11 and 12 especially impressed me. In those verses are these words: "For he shall give his angels charge over thee, to keep thee in all thy ways. They shall bear thee up in their hands, lest thou dash thy foot against a stone" (KJV).

I believe God answered my prayer through that passage. Psalm 91 told me that the fisherman was my guardian angel.

As told by Scott Yost.
First published in Signs of the Times, *May 1999.*
Used by permission.

CHAPTER 5

The Brush of Angel Wings

Anyone who's lived in Scottsdale, Arizona, knows how blistering hot summers can be there. My husband and I were living in a mobile home at the edge of the campus of Thunderbird Academy. To the north, the desert stretched for miles.

One hot afternoon, I strolled toward our garden located between our home and the furniture factory. Heat waves danced around me. I stooped to turn on the faucet. "Ouch!" I said aloud. "That tap is scorching hot!" I blew at my fingers. "I wonder how hot it is out here? Guess I'd best water our garden, if I want it to survive," I told myself. Hose in hand, I moved from row to row, soaking everything. Just as I finished watering, I felt a slight touch like something faintly brushing my back, causing an unusual sensation. Startled, I turned to see what had touched me.

When I turned, I saw Mr. Fritz, one of the academy teachers, standing there staring at me with dazed eyes.

"Mr. Fritz! What are you doing here?" I began. "Your T-shirt is covered with blood! Your face is skinned! Your eyebrow is cut!" He did not reply.

"Put your arm around my shoulder, Mr. Fritz. You must be badly hurt!" I practically carried him to our house and sat him in a lawn chair.

"I'll call your wife and the school nurse," I told him.

"Am I married?" he asked.

"Yes, you're married. Now, tell me what have you been up to?"

"Riding my motorcycle," he said.

While waiting for the school nurse, Mr. Fritz told me he remembered replacing the spark plug and putting new points in his motorcycle. But because he planned to take the bike for just a short test drive, he did not wear his helmet nor long pants. "The last thing I remember," he said, "is leaving the house for the test drive."

The school nurse arrived and immediately took him to the hospital, where he remained for twenty-four hours.

When my husband came home from work, I told him about Mr. Fritz's unusual appearance in our garden. "I'll walk out to the desert and see if I can find the motorcycle," my husband said. After a cold drink of water, he walked a mile to where he thought our friend might have been riding his motorcycle. He found the bike. All around it he saw markings in the sand indicating the rider had crawled around struggling to get up. However, he saw no other foot prints in the dirt.

After my husband arrived home with the bike, he said, "I wonder how he ever got up off that hot ground? And you say you could barely get him to the house?"

"That's right! I practically carried him from the garden."

"Then how did he get to our garden from the desert?"

Then I remembered that something had brushed my back while I was watering the garden, causing me to turn around and see Mr. Fritz. I told my husband about the strange sensation. He went to the place I had been standing, but he found no footprints in the mud—other than mine and those of Mr. Fritz.

Because one may dehydrate quickly in the hot desert, I believe Mr. Fritz's guardian angel carried him to the nearest human help available—me, watering our garden. I believe I felt the brush of angel wings on my back to get my attention so that I could quickly obtain help. I believe we will have to wait until heaven to understand how often our lives have been involved with the ministry of heavenly angels and how often they have intervened in our behalf.

As told by Gladys Dickerson and Gottfried Fritz.
First published by He's Alive, Volume 11, Numbers 3, 4.
Used by permission.

CHAPTER 6

God Sent Someone

In 1959, I had just completed four years of service in the navy. Fortunately, I got a job at my future brother-in-law's gas station in Manteca, California. At that time I was dating Gwen, a former Seventh-day Adventist Christian. Gwen had attended Lodi Academy; however, she stopped attending church after graduation. I was brought up in the Roman Catholic faith and occasionally attended mass while I was in the navy.

Several nights a week, after closing the gas station at 8:00 P.M., I would drive to Lodi to see Gwen. Often those evening visits lasted until late, and I fought sleep on the way home to Manteca. Many times I pulled off on the shoulder of the road and slept a while before driving the rest of the way home.

One evening, I closed the station at the usual time and turned off the outside lights. Instead of visiting Gwen, I decided to work on my 1937 Chevy coupe. I drove the car into the garage and pulled it up just far enough for the hoist to catch the front bumper. I raised the car high enough to crawl underneath and began trying to loosen a bolt connected to the suspension system. I didn't realize that the car wasn't sitting straight on the hoist, but at a slight angle. Also, I hadn't raised the hoist high enough for the safety lock to drop into place. As I applied pressure on the bolt I was trying to loosen, the hoist suddenly began coming down, and the car landed squarely on my chest!

Frantically, I struggled to get out from beneath the car as it slowly descended with the hoist, but I wasn't able to get free. I quickly reached for the tire I had just removed; I tried to drag it under the wheel drum and stop the car from settling further, but the tire was too heavy to move in my position. Gradually, the car kept coming down with the hoist. As its weight pressed on my chest, I thought, *If I don't get help quickly, I'm going to be crushed to death!*

"Help me! Someone, please, help me!" I yelled. Then I added, "Oh, God, please help me!" I don't remember how long it was after I'd asked for God's help, but all at once I saw, from my horizontal position under the car, a pair of man's legs walk into the garage.

"Push that lever up!" I shouted. "The one over there!"

My arms were straining to push the car away from my chest. I saw the legs walk over to the hoist lever on the wall. Slowly, the car began moving upward! Gasping for breath, I managed to roll from under the vehicle.

For a few moments I knelt on the garage floor, rubbing my chest. Then still looking down, I said aloud, "I thought I was going to die right there under my car!" I turned to thank the person who had raised the hoist and saved my life—but I couldn't see anyone in the room. *Where did that man disappear to so quickly?* I thought to myself.

I continued sitting on the floor, taking one deep breath after another. A woman walked into the lighted garage from the darkness outside. "May I buy some gas?" she asked. "My car is so low on fuel I'm afraid to travel much farther without buying gas." Then, seeing that I was still gasping for air and holding my chest, she asked, "Are you all right?"

Between breaths, I told her what had just happened. She looked surprised. "I didn't see anyone come out of the station as I walked in," she said.

"I saw a man's pants and shoes walking around the car," I told her. "He raised the car off my chest and saved my life." Both of us walked out the door and around the garage, looking for the man who saved me, but no one was in sight anywhere!

At that point in my life, I didn't realize what had taken place that night. When I visited Gwen the next evening and told her what had happened, she said, "It could have been an angel who saved you!"

I shrugged my shoulders. "Whoever it was, he saved my life!"

I'll never forget what happened that night in that garage in Manteca, California. Years later, I became a Christian. Now I know God sent someone into that garage that night when I was in desperate need of help. Whether the man who rescued me was a heavenly angel or an earthly man, I still don't know. But I know I'm alive today because God heard my desperate prayer for help that night and spared my life. I can never thank Him enough!

As told by Tom Baker.

CHAPTER 7

Delayed Answer

Rick rolled over and opened his eyes. The early morning sunlight streamed through the bedroom window. A quick glance toward his cousin Delvin's bed assured Rick that he wasn't the last one to wake up.

"Hey, Delvin, wake up and enjoy a brand-new day!"

Delvin groaned, "Why are you such an early bird? Leave me alone and let me sleep some more."

A pillow landed squarely on Delvin's mop of brown hair.

"OK, OK," he muttered. "Mom will be calling soon, anyway." With a sudden burst of energy he sprang out of bed. "I'll race you! I'll bet I can get dressed and ready for breakfast before you."

During breakfast Rick remarked, "Let's see, tomorrow my three-day vacation will end. You're lucky people to live out in the woods in a place like this!" Turning to Delvin's father, he asked, "You don't have a tree you need to cut down while I'm here, do you?"

"As a matter of fact, I do," his uncle responded, "but there's a problem. It's so near the property line that before I cut it down, I have to make sure it's really my tree."

Delvin spoke up, "There'd be a shooting if we cut it down and our completely irrational neighbor found that even a quarter inch of it was on his property!"

"Now, Delvin, that's stretching things a bit too far," his mother cautioned.

"Well, he wouldn't stop short of suing us," Delvin countered.

Rick broke in, "Will you have to hire a surveyor?"

"No," his uncle assured him. "The two corner stakes are there. We just need to clear away enough brush to be able to sight from one stake to the other."

"How big a job is it?" Rick asked.

"A couple hours should handle it if we work hard and fast."

"OK, let's get at it!" Rick pushed his chair back from the table and gave Delvin an encouraging slap on the shoulder.

Soon the sound of axes could be heard. Clumps of underbrush and branches were dragged into a clearing and stacked for future burning.

"When we get over this rise just ahead," Delvin told Rick, "we can look down toward the other corner stake where Dad is working. Once we clear enough brush for him to see us, we can cut down the tree without having bullets whizzing past us!"

"We must have really been working hard," Rick said. "You're dad said it would take two hours, and we haven't been working that long." He pushed up his jacket sleeve to check the time. "Oh no!" he exclaimed. "My watch is gone!"

"You've got to be kidding," Delvin flashed an appraising glance back over the area they had cleared. "It would be next to impossible to find it out here in this deep litter of leaves and sticks."

But Rick wasn't kidding. His watch was gone. The boys began searching; Delvin's parents joined in. But to no avail.

"I'm convinced it would take nothing short of a metal detector—more likely, an outright miracle—to locate that watch in all this debris," Delvin's father said. Nevertheless, the search continued.

Later, while eating lunch, Rick questioned, "Is there still time before evening to sight along the property line and cut down the tree?"

His uncle smiled. "That would be a double tragedy, wouldn't it—for you to lose your watch *and* miss out on felling the tree? Sure, we'll get it down all right."

The tree came down, and watching it fall was just as exciting as Rick had hoped it would be.

After supper that evening, Delvin announced, "I've got an idea. Maybe your watch got hung up on some of those branches we carried to the burning pile this morning. Let's tear that pile apart and look over each branch."

"OK!" Rick responded eagerly.

Soon both boys were energetically dismantling the stack of brush.

"I once heard of a kid who lost some of his father's war medals in the woods," Delvin said. "A woman who was helping him look for them suggested there was Someone who knew exactly where those medals were, so why not ask Him for help? They did, and it wasn't long until they found them."

Rick, a branch poised in midair, looked squarely into Delvin's eyes. "Maybe you think I haven't been doing some praying about this."

"I'm sure you have, Rick. It may look like our prayers aren't being answered. But maybe God is just testing our faith."

The next morning when the family took Rick to the airport, Delvin's parting words were, "Keep right on praying that the watch will show up, and I'll go right on searching."

And he kept that promise. As soon as he got home, Delvin started going over the same area the family had searched before. "Talk about looking for a needle in a haystack," he muttered as he looked, "well, this is a match for it! I'd call myself an idiot for wasting my time this way if we hadn't prayed for help."

A half hour passed. Delvin needed to do other chores, but he didn't want to call it quits. "Lord," he prayed, "You know it's impossible to find Rick's watch without Your help. You know, too, that I should be helping Dad. Please lead me to the watch soon."

Looking around him once more, Delvin noticed some stray branches he and Rick hadn't carried off the day before. "Might as well gather them up," he said to himself. "They sure don't enhance the scenery much anyway. Maybe I'll catch sight of the watch between here and the burn pile."

Returning for a second armload, he stopped short. "No, siree! No way!" he declared decisively. Directly in front of him—on the neighbor's side of the dividing line—lay two small branches. *Since the neighbor is so fussy about trespassers, he can keep those branches,* Delvin thought. *It'll serve him right.*

31

But then he had second thoughts. *Of course, it's our fault they are there.*

He reached for the nearest branch. As he did so, something to the left of it caught his eye. There it was! Rick's watch lay right at the base of the tree from which the two branches had been cut. Delvin felt conscience-stricken. He thought, *How come none of us was able to spot that watch before? It was only after I showed some consideration for our unhappy neighbor that I saw it.* Before making another move he breathed the words, "Lord, forgive me for my unkind thoughts."

Kneeling down, Delvin took the watch into his hands. "Thank You, Lord," he whispered. "And thank You for testing my faith."

Written by Mabel Latsha.
First published by Guide, Volume 24, Number 38.
Used by permission.

CHAPTER 8

Down the Steep Mountainside

Twenty-five degrees below zero made it a cold Thanksgiving morning as I drove with two of my co-workers down a rough Forest Service road to our tree-felling job about eighty miles from Boise, Idaho. Comfortably seated in my full-size Ford pickup, with four-wheel drive and only four thousand miles on the odometer, we were nearing the top of a mountain range in the Sawtooth Wilderness area. At an elevation of 6,500 feet, there was snow on the road.

As we came to a sharp curve near the summit, the rear of my pickup began to slide toward the canyon. I was going only ten or fifteen miles per hour, but I noticed that the road slanted left toward the canyon rather than right toward the mountain. I kept all four wheels pulling and steered the front end of the pickup toward the mountain, praying all the while that the all-weather tires would find traction. As our forward motion came almost to a stop, the pickup spun completely around, slid off the road, and rolled twice down the steep mountainside. There was nothing I could do but pray as we plunged downward.

Miraculously, the pickup came to rest right side up on top of a low snag! Carefully assessing the situation, we found that the frame of the pickup was balanced on the snag. The left wheels were on the mountainside, and the right wheels dangled in midair. The window glass of the passenger door was gone, and my co-worker next to the door was unconscious, his right arm hanging out of the open window.

Cautiously, my conscious co-worker, seated in the middle of the cab, crawled through the broken window and dropped below the pickup. Then he climbed up beside the driver's door to help me pull it open.

Fortunately, two other vehicles from our crew were behind us. One had a telephone and called a search-and-rescue helicopter. We waited, but the helicopter never found the site of the wreck. Finally, we decided to call a logging helicopter in the vicinity. It came with a stretcher, to which we tied our unconscious co-worker. Then six of us struggled to get him to the helicopter. We expected to hear that he had severe neck or spinal injuries, but when he arrived at the hospital, doctors could find no major problems, and he was discharged within twenty-four hours! My other co-worker and I received a few bruises, but we didn't even lose work over the mishap!

A heavy-duty wrecker arrived to winch the pickup off the snag. We were surprised to find that all the chain saws and gas cans in the pickup bed had stayed inside the canopy; only a few small items had flown out. None of the gas cans were punctured, and none of the gas had spilled. I was also happy to discover that my pickup had suffered a relatively small amount of damage. One window in the canopy had popped out, so I had to buy a new canopy. The front fenders and the pickup bed also had to be replaced. On January 14, I got my pickup out of the shop. It looked like a brand-new vehicle, and when driving it, I could not detect a sprung frame or any difference in operation.

I know God guided my pickup down the mountainside. If we had missed that one snag, we could have rolled from a half to three-fourths of a mile down that precipitous mountainside, possibly to our deaths because there were no other trees large enough to stop the truck. I thank the Lord for saving our lives on Thanksgiving Day 1993.

As told by Ron Roberts. Written by Wes Roberts.
First published by He's Alive, *Volume 5, Number 6.*
Used by permission.

CHAPTER 9

In the Clutches of a Blizzard

My wife, Bertha, our two-year-old son, Jerry, and I were heading for the home farm in Alberta, Canada, in the middle of a snowstorm. It was snowing fairly hard when we reached the familiar town of Beiseker, only thirteen miles from the farm. Having lived in Canada a few years, I was accustomed to snowy weather and felt confident we could make it to the farm if the storm didn't become worse.

Prairie side roads in Canada don't have road markers. You find your way by mileage and by observing physical features. Someone might tell you, "Go five miles east and turn south at the two granaries; then go three miles, and you will come to a red barn."

Shortly after we left Beiseker, the snowstorm turned into a ferocious blizzard. The strong winds whipped the falling snow into a whiteout. We couldn't see a thing and were in a life-threatening predicament. Bertha and I agreed that our only hope was to trust God. He knew where we were and where we wanted to go. We were constantly in an attitude of prayer.

We knew what to look for in order to find the road to the farm—an automobile tire mounted on an eight-foot pole with the words "Gramm's Corner" painted on it in white letters. A neighbor had erected this unique sign at the corner of the highway and the road to help people find his farm. With God's help, if we could find that tire in the storm, we would have only five more miles to go. We continued to pray that God would help us find that sign.

Our car crept along the highway as we kept our eyes on the edges of the road. If the car drifted to the right side of the road, my wife would yell, "ditch!" I, in turn, watched through the blinding snow for the ditch on the left. We had to keep going because snow drifts would block the road in a short time and trap us.

For eight torturous miles I drove at a snail's pace, frightfully tense while trying to steer the car between the ditches. If we ran into a ditch, our situation would be extremely critical. The temperature was about twenty degrees below zero, and I knew the amount of gas in the car wouldn't keep the motor running to keep the heat on through the night.

Peering out the window, trying to see something familiar, I said to Bertha, "We must be very close to the Gramm's tire."

"I think so," she replied.

Our odometer told us we'd better stop or we would miss the corner to our road. We sat peering in the direction where we knew Gramm's tire sign must be. In anticipation and expectation we stared into the blizzard, believing by faith that God would show us the tire. I could see nothing but the driving snow carried on the wings of the powerful gale. I anxiously waited. Suddenly a mysterious blast of wind opened a hole in the tempestuous storm.

There it was—Gramm's tire! The moment was absolutely unbelievable. We could now see the place we needed to turn onto the road that would lead us home. We weren't more than fifty feet from the corner, but we still had five miles to go.

God is absolutely incredible and awesome beyond words! I believe He had a powerful angel hold back the fierce storm for a few seconds so that we could see the sign and know where to go. The pole and tire at our corner remained visible until we turned and drove south.

Then just as suddenly as the lull in the storm had appeared, it disappeared! The thirty-mile-an-hour wind whipped up in fury again with a resulting whiteout. Driving the last five miles to the farm seemed almost overwhelming, as though every devil on the planet wanted to destroy us. Snowdrifts formed on the road, making it even harder to see the ditches.

About half a mile from the farm, there was a small valley to go through—a place where snowdrifts accumulated. I could sense that Bertha's anxiety matched my own as we approached that spot in the road. Could we make it through? I gripped the steering wheel, praying as I stepped on the gas pedal and plummeted through the drifts. I don't know how we made it out of that valley, but I believe angels helped us.

Now our last big obstacle—where was the driveway? As if we didn't have enough apprehension, it was starting to get dark. I knew dangers still lay ahead, and recalled hearing about farmers getting lost between their houses and barns. We inched along about half a mile, peering into the driving snow for some sign of the corner fence post that marked the entrance to the driveway. The entrance had a post on one side with a chain wrapped around it. This was the Grabo signature so that people could find the farm.

Again we prayed, "Father, one more time. Please save us." I remember how we stared with great expectation, trusting that God would open a spot in the storm as He did on the highway. With majestic power, He directed a gust of wind to encircle the fence post, holding back the fury of the blizzard so that the only quiet spot in the storm was around the fence post with the identifying chain wrapped around it!

Due to God's guiding hand we turned into the driveway and immediately plowed into a deep snowdrift; the gallant car gave up, refusing to go any farther.

We struggled to get the car doors open against the deep snow. It seemed like all the demons in the world were trying to squeeze out all of the hideous circumstances they could muster against us. Our last struggle for survival had begun. We must find the farmhouse, which, like most homes on the prairie, was set back from the road.

The blowing snow stung our faces, making it hard to see. There was no fence on the north side of the road, only open wheat fields. If we wandered out into the open field, we would no doubt perish. But God still had His watchful eye on us. We prayed constantly as we struggled through the snow; in some places it was up to our hips. We took turns carrying our small son, and I had to be careful to follow the south fence line—our lifeline.

I couldn't see a thing in the whiteout, only Bertha beside me. This taught me the frustration that a blind person must feel. Knowing the farmyard by heart, I located familiar objects as we stumbled on them. Then suddenly, I saw the outline of the house.

We pushed open the door and entered, stomping the snow off our shoes and clothes.

The folks were astonished, bombarding us with questions, "Where did you come from? How did you get here? Are you all right?" It seemed unbelievable that we had made it to the farm through the raging storm.

Later a number of people in the neighborhood said, "That blizzard was one of the worst we have had for a long time. By rights, you shouldn't have made it to the farm in that storm with all the snow that was on the roads."

By rights, we shouldn't have. But God specializes in the impossible. He is absolutely amazing. He knows where we live and where we are at all times—even in the clutches of a blizzard.

Written by Donald Palmer and Mort Juberg.
First published by **He's Alive,** *Volume 11, Numbers 3, 4.*
Used by permission.

CHAPTER 10

Dream Guidance

One summer my father hired a man to move our mobile home from Yuba City, California, to Moses Lake, Washington. My father and teenage brother then returned to California to continue working. After they earned more money, they planned to come back to Washington and bring the rest of our belongings.

While mother unpacked and organized our trailer into a home, my sister and I enjoyed playing outdoors. Throughout the summer, we lived in Moses Lake without Dad and our brother. We looked forward to the day when the whole family could be reunited.

After two months, Dad called Mother one morning and said, "It looks like we're not going to be able to come up just yet."

"Why?" mother asked. "What's happened?"

"I lost my money," he replied. "I can't understand what happened. I hid all the money I had saved somewhere . . . and I can't remember where I put it!"

"That's terrible!" Mother exclaimed. "Think hard; maybe you'll remember what you did with it."

"I've thought and thought. I just can't remember. Now, we'll have to keep working a while longer and save more money before we can come home."

After the phone call, Mother turned to us and said, "I have bad news, girls. Dad isn't coming home just yet."

"Why?" I asked.

"Because he misplaced his money and can't remember where he put it. I think we should pray," she stated with determination. The three of us knelt and asked God, "Please help Dad remember where he put that money so that he won't have to work any longer before he can come home."

All day at school I kept thinking about my father and his lost money. That night before I climbed into bed, I prayed most earnestly, "Please, dear Jesus, help Dad remember where he put that money." Dad and I were close, and I missed him a great deal. Now it could possibly take another two or three months before he and my brother could join us. Even after I crawled under the covers, I kept thinking about Dad. I continued asking the Lord to help my father find the money so that he could come home soon.

Finally, I fell asleep. That night, in my dreams, I saw my father take his money, roll it up, and stuff it into an old shoe. In my dream I saw him walk around the house with the old shoe in hand looking for somewhere to hide it. I saw him carry the shoe to his bedroom and throw it under the bed.

The next morning, I awoke giggling. I bounced out of bed and raced to the kitchen. "Mother, I had a silly dream last night," I exclaimed. "I saw Dad put that money in one of his old shoes and throw it under his bed." Both my mother and my sister joined me in laughing at my dream.

The school year had just begun, so mother hurried us out the door saying, "You'd best run off to school or you'll be late."

Arriving home after school, we saw Mother standing in the doorway waiting for us. Usually we would burst through the door, calling to her—eager to tell her about our day at school. We raced toward her, thinking something was wrong.

Worried, I asked, "What's up?"

"You'd best come in and sit down," she announced. "I've got something to tell you." The first thing that came to my mind was that something had happened to Dad!

We sat down; Mother had our full attention. Tears moistened her eyes as she spoke. "Barbara, remember the dream you had last night? As silly as that dream seemed, I decided because we'd prayed about the lost money, I should call Dad and tell him your dream. Maybe the Lord gave you that dream to help him find his money. When I called Dad and told him your dream, he immediately remembered what he'd done. He thought that if anyone broke into the house, they'd never look in an old shoe for money."

Because of my dream, my father and brother came home within one week. Once again we became a happy, united family.

I've often wondered why the Lord gave me that dream. Was it because I continued to pray late into the night that Dad would find his money? After that, God became very real to me—a little ten-year-old, fourth-grade girl. That experience built in me a strong faith in God's love, care, and guidance that has sustained me through many of life's trials.

As told by Barbara Dunston-LaRose.
First published by **Adventist** Review, *April 25, 2002.*
Used by permission.

CHAPTER 11

Our Family's Unusual Guest

About 1925, in the north-central part of South Dakota, our widowed mother lived on a farm with her three sons, aged five, eight, and fourteen. In that community everybody knew everybody for miles around. The surrounding farmers not only knew every person but also recognized their neighbors' horses, wagons, and machinery.

Late one autumn day, a wagon with a lone driver approached our farm through the pasture. There was nothing unusual about his going through our pasture; neighbors often used the pasture roads as a shortcut to haul grain and produce to town. What made this approach unusual was that a mule team—not horses—pulled the wagon. We were certain that no one in our surrounding area owned mules!

The driver guided his fine-looking mule team into our yard and politely asked Mother, "Ma'am, may I please find lodging here for the night?"

Since Mother hesitated to answer, the stranger added, "I'll be happy to sleep in the hay loft and just use a little hay for my mules!"

Mother thought a moment longer. She was afraid that if the man smoked, he might set our hay barn on fire. Finally she said, "Boys, help the man unhitch his mules and give them some hay. I'll fix a bed for him on the floor in the summer kitchen."

In those days most farm homes had a summer kitchen. In these summer kitchens, housewives canned fruit and vegetables from their gardens. Summer kitchens also served as the family laundry room.

Soon after the mules were fed, the darkness of night engulfed us. The stranger was shown to his bed in the summer kitchen, and the family retired for the night in the house. Early the next morning the family arose to visit with their guest. But to their surprise the stranger, his wagon, and the mules were gone! We asked several neighbors if they'd seen the stranger with his wagon pulled by mules. No one in the surrounding neighborhood saw him arrive or leave our yard!

Who was this mysterious stranger? Everyone wanted to know! We were convinced that this visitor was most likely an angel who had come to check out the hospitality of our home. Or perhaps he protected our fatherless family from some unknown harm while we slept. Hopefully, some day we'll meet this angelic guest in heaven, where he can explain the reason for his visit to our home.

Mother often quoted Hebrews 13:2. "Be not forgetful to entertain strangers: for thereby some have entertained angels unawares" (KJV).

As told by F. W. Bieber.

CHAPTER 12

Imitating an Angel

When my mother came from upstate New York for a visit, we planned a summer family picnic to celebrate. I, my husband, our sons, ages ten and twelve, and my mother all packed our picnic baskets and drove to a natural park to enjoy our family afternoon together.

After our picnic lunch, my husband and the boys decided to go for a walk in the surrounding woods. Mother and I relaxed and visited at our picnic area. Our boys are exuberant, lively children. About a half hour later I heard excited voices as they neared the picnic area. I looked up and saw the boys running pell-mell down a false path toward the deep ravine which separated us. They'd left their father behind to enjoy his walk alone.

I panicked! A few more steps, and they'd tumble headlong into the ravine. Frozen with fear, I was unable to scream a warning. They likely wouldn't have heard me anyhow.

Just then, out of the corner of my eye, I saw a figure standing on our side of the ravine and to my right. He wore a long, off-white, tunic-type garment—similar to a choir robe. He faced the boys, arm outstretched and hand in a "stop" position—like a policeman would do. The second I saw that man, I quickly imitated his hand signal to my sons. The boys looked up just in time, saw my signal, and slid to an immediate stop inches from the ravine's edge! Had the figure appeared brilliant, he would have diverted my attention from the boys, and I likely would have missed giving them the "stop" signal in time to save them from untold injuries or even death!

Always well-behaved boys, our sons stopped immediately upon my signal! I wasn't surprised at that; they usually obeyed promptly. After they stopped, they looked down into the deep, dry ravine. Then they turned, discovered the true path which ran parallel to the ravine, and scampered down that path. Now that my boys were safe, I looked to where the man had stood, intending to thank him for his help in saving my boys from falling headlong into the ravine. But he was nowhere in sight!

I collapsed in exhaustion and relief! The boy's narrow escape had upset me. Pointing, I asked my mother, "Did you see that man standing over there at the edge of the ravine signaling for the boys to stop?" She did not reply because she was in shock after watching what had just happened.

As I recovered from the fright my sons gave me, I realized that the unusually dressed figure who gave me the stop signal to imitate was none other than their guardian angel!

As told by Judith Stein.

CHAPTER 13

Angel Intervention

One cold January morning, I drew back the drapes to analyze the weather. "It looks frigid out there!" I told my daughter, Lila, who'd been visiting me for a few days.

"I know, the weather isn't the best, Mother," she scurried to collect her last few possessions and quickly packed them into her already full suitcase, "but I have to catch the plane out of Spokane at noon today."

"We'd better leave soon to allow extra time," I suggested. "It takes nearly three hours to get to Spokane on good roads. Today, the roads north of here could be icy."

Hastily, Lila snapped the suitcase lid shut. "I'm ready to go whenever you are, Mother." Quickly, we loaded the car. I hopped behind the wheel, and we drove northward. All went well until we neared the little town of Colfax.

"That's the second car I've seen in the ditch," I said, pointing. "I guess I should slow down even more."

Those words had barely escaped my lips, when we encountered a wide curve to the left. The car hit black ice, slid across the road, and plunged into a three-foot ditch. We came to a stop with a terrible thud!

While sliding, I had noticed a culvert and a gravel road about twenty feet ahead, which led to a farmhouse, nestled about three hundred yards from the highway. After the impact, we opened our eyes and discovered our car was no longer in the ditch, but resting lengthwise across the culvert! The width of the culvert and the length of our car were exactly the same. At the time, we didn't stop to wonder or ask ourselves how our car moved from the ditch to the culvert in the blink of an eye. We had more important things to think about. "How are you going to get to the airport in time to catch your plane?" I asked Lila.

"Are you all right, Mother?" Lila asked. "I'm not hurt."

"I think I'm OK, but I feel numb." As we sat there a few minutes pondering what to do next, a truck stopped. The driver ran toward our car.

"Are you ladies all right?" He asked as Lila rolled down her window.

"I'm OK, but Mother feels numb."

"I'll call the Colfax ambulance and wrecker, if you wish," he offered.

"OK!" Lila said.

The man called the ambulance and a wrecker on his portable phone. Soon the ambulance whisked us toward the Colfax hospital.

"Where were you ladies headed?" the ambulance driver asked.

"Mother was taking me to the Spokane airport to catch the noon plane for home," Lila replied.

"Don't worry! I'm going that way immediately and can drop you off at the airport on my way to Spokane. You'll still be able to catch your flight in time," the driver said as he glanced at his watch.

"Thank you, so much!" Lila answered. We were both relieved that she would still make it to the airport on time.

At the hospital, X-rays revealed I had a center-back compression fracture. I remained hospitalized for three days. Friends came to take me home. After about six weeks of rest at home, friends took me to Colfax to retrieve my car.

The first thing the mechanic said to me was, "How in the world did your car get up on the culvert? I saw your tire marks in the ditch, and there was no place it could have climbed out of that ditch! Besides," he continued, "your left front wheel was twisted halfway around, so there is no way your car could have gotten to the culvert on its own power!"

"The only answer, I can give you," I responded, "is that our guardian angel must have picked up our car from the ditch and placed it crosswise on the culvert!"

He shook his head in disbelief! I quoted Psalm 34:7 to him, "The angel of the LORD encampeth round about them that fear him, and delivereth them" (KJV).

He still stood there shaking his head. But I believe that is just what happened. Even today, it's a great comfort to me to think that our guardian angels traveled with us on that icy road.

As told by Grace Streifling.

CHAPTER 14

Three Gathered in My Name

Sleepily, I snatched the receiver off the hook as the phone rang persistently early on a cold December morning. "Hello."

"Hi Mom, I'm so excited. I've been chosen as one of our college group to go on a study tour to Central America in January. We're to stay there five months and learn the language!"

Suddenly wide-awake, I said, "But Anne, haven't you heard of all the political unrest in Central America? The newspapers are filled with stories about the Jesuit priests killed there recently! Are you sure you want to go on this trip?"

"Don't worry, Mom, God will take care of our group," Anne assured me.

Reluctantly, I hung up the phone and shared the news with my husband. Thoughts of concern for Anne and her group's safety while in Central America churned in my mind all day. I shared my concerns with a friend, and during the next few weeks, the two of us prayed for Anne's safety and for the group she was traveling with. Every Thursday afternoon I met with a prayer group at our church altar. I shared my concern with my assembled prayer friends. One particular Thursday I knelt in the midst of two other women, praying aloud about private requests and world conditions. Momentarily I fell silent. Then suddenly I heard myself say, "Thank You, God, for protecting Anne with Your angels!" The two women beside me gasped, and each confessed, "Judy, the same words you just prayed came to my mind at the same time you spoke them!" The three of us looked at each other in surprise; we couldn't figure out what was going on.

One lady said, "This is like a special holy moment. To think that the three of us thought to make the identical prayer request at the same time!"

"This is unusual!" I replied. I'm not a person who generally thinks of angels. Nor am I constantly aware of them protecting people. So the fact that those words came out of my mouth the way they did seemed very unusual.

After that experience, I promptly wrote Anne and asked if anything unusual happened during the time we were praying for her at the church altar. Anne was in a different time zone, so she would have to compute the time difference in order to determine what was happening to her during our prayer session.

Anne replied to my letter confirming that she had been involved in a scary situation at the exact time of our prayer session at the church altar. She kept a daily journal and had recorded that strange experience. She also told me later that many times she'd felt uneasy due to the political unrest in that area. While in Nicaragua, their group often heard gun shots. People screamed at them because they were Americans. In Guatemala they saw soldiers on the roofs of buildings with guns poised ready to shoot. One weekend their group hiked to a volcano and learned later that guerrillas had overtaken that same area the following week. A month or two after they left Guatemala City, they heard that the streets were filled with tanks!

On the particular day of our unusual prayer session, Anne was in the city of Antigua Guatemala. She and a friend were late leaving the language class to get lunch. The last students to leave, they had walked out of the school and across the street, when a man stopped them. Hysterically, he began describing assassinations he'd witnessed. He kept repeating that they were the only ones who could help him. From his disjointed talk, they wondered if he was on drugs.

"I left my motorcycle under the cross that overlooks the city," he pointed. "I need you to get some gas for my motorcycle, so I can leave town as soon as possible." He told them he was from El Salvador and had just arrived in Guatemala. "I need directions how to get out of town." He rambled on with a lot of details that didn't make sense. They couldn't figure out why he kept saying they were the only ones who could help him.

Their professors had instructed them not to talk to strangers due to the political unrest in that area. Anne remembered, too, that I had taught her the same thing all her life. They were young, Americans, and barely knew Spanish. There were other signs that made them wonder what was really behind this man's continuous conversation. Was he legitimate or not? Anne still doesn't know the answer to that question.

While the man continued to talk, Anne and her friend looked down the street and saw about thirty uniformed Guatemalan soldiers marching toward them. When the man saw the soldiers, he became very nervous. "We've got to get out of here!" he said. He dashed behind a building and hid. Anne and her friend never saw him again. Nor did they have to come up with an excuse as to why they could not help him. They quietly retraced their steps and went back inside the school. In their hurry, they left the door—a large, twelve-foot slab of wood—open. Looking out, they saw the soldiers still coming up the street. As the soldiers drew even with the door, it slammed shut all by itself. There was no one near the door; there was no breeze. They felt a protection they could not explain.

Later, we determined that the exact time that the door swung shut was the time my two friends and I were earnestly praying back in the state of Washington for Anne's safety. Later that year Anne returned home safely! God's angels had indeed protected Anne while she was in Central America. We don't understand much about this particular experience, but we know that God intervened in answer to our prayers. After all, He has promised, "For where two or three are gathered together in my name, there am I in the midst of them" (Matthew 18:20, KJV).

As told by Judy Goranson.

CHAPTER 15

Late-Night Rescue

A few days before Thanksgiving in 1940, we planned a trip to Kansas to attend a family reunion. We planned to drive straight through to Kansas from our home in Arlington, Washington, just north of Seattle. We invited Leonard's brother, Carl, and Carl's new wife, LaVolla, to come with us as extra drivers. After we packed our luggage into our 1930 Model A sedan, we made a bed on top of the luggage with warm blankets so that some of us could rest while the others remained awake to drive. With our two young children, there were six of us in all.

Leonard secured sturdy cardboard in front of the radiator to protect it from freezing while we drove through below-zero temperatures en route. We arrived in Salt Lake City without any problems. From there we had planned to drive across Colorado. But when we heard that the main highway through Colorado had been closed due to a snowstorm, we decided to take an alternate route through Wyoming.

While in Salt Lake City, we noticed the gas gauge was getting low, but we drove around the Mormon temple downtown and enjoyed the sights, planning to get gas as we left the city. However, it was late—near midnight—when we finally left. The gas gauge hovered near "Empty." We searched for an open gas station, but found none. For two hours, we crawled along the snowy highway, but met no traffic.

"Surely, we'll find a gas station soon," Leonard reassured us. We drove for miles, but found nothing open. As the gas gauge needle crept to "E," the temperature outdoors plunged below zero. Wind-driven snow cascaded continually across the highway. We strained our eyes searching for farmhouse lights. In the distance, we saw only the lights of a speeding passenger train. Slowly our car lumbered to a stop.

"Wish we were all on the warm train, instead of stranded here on this cold, snowy road," LaVolla mused aloud.

"Look! There's a light ahead," Leonard shouted. "It could be some road equipment at work. Carl, let's walk toward the light and ask where the nearest filling station is." The men had just crawled out of the car when suddenly a Buick pulled up beside them. A man jumped out and asked, "Are you in trouble?"

"We're out of gas," Leonard said.

"Do you have anyone in the car with you?"

"Yes, two ladies and two children," Leonard told him.

"We can't leave them here for long. They'll freeze to death," the stranger said. "Do you have antifreeze in your radiator?" he quickly asked.

"Not much," Leonard replied, "it's mostly water."

"Drain it, or it'll freeze and ruin your car!" While Leonard drained the radiator, the stranger paced back and forth in the blizzard as though pondering what to do next. "Do you have a tow rope?" he asked.

"All I have is a pair of tire chains."

"Get them!" he urged. Leonard got the chains, and the men fastened them together. Next they attached them to the Buick's back bumper and to our car's front bumper. Shivering, Leonard and Carl jumped into the front seat, while the rest of us cuddled under blankets in the back. Our car eased forward. In spite of the icy road, the Buick towed us steadily for six miles without slipping once. Then the driver pulled us into an open gas station.

Greatly relieved, we all crawled out and walked into the warm building. As though he were familiar with the surroundings, our rescuer pointed, "Ladies, the restroom is over there." Before he led the men to their restroom, he told the service attendant, "These folks need gas! They also need antifreeze in their radiator."

After the service man had attended to our car, Leonard paid him for the gas and antifreeze. Then Carl and Leonard searched the station and looked outdoors for the kind stranger, but neither he nor his Buick were anywhere in sight.

Extremely thankful, we arrived safely at our destination for the family reunion. We gratefully celebrated Thanksgiving and thanked God for the kind stranger who saved us from freezing to death in that Wyoming blizzard. Often we've wondered if he was a human angel or a heavenly angel! Someday we'll learn what kind of angel rescued us that night. Meanwhile, we know that "the angel of the LORD encampeth round about them that fear him, and delivereth them" (Psalm 34:7, KJV).

As told by Leonard, Wilma, and LaVolla Dickerson.

CHAPTER 16

Escape From Invisible Poison

In September 1984, I accepted a teaching position at Campion Academy in Colorado, and we moved into the oldest house on the campus. Later that month, I winterized the house by sealing old exhaust flues and putting in storm windows. During mid-October, the first snow fell. The weather turned cold, and the furnace ran constantly.

About this time, my in-laws passed through the area and stayed overnight at our house. The next morning, my mother-in-law awoke with a severe headache. Our two daughters didn't feel well either.

"I hurt all over, Mommy!" our youngest daughter claimed.

"I ache all over, too!" our eldest daughter added.

"After a good breakfast you'll all feel better," my wife told the girls.

When my in-laws left, my wife and youngest daughter went with them to Minnesota. Meanwhile, the weather turned colder, and more snow fell. The two older children and I attended school each day. We spent only evenings and nights at home. All of us complained of slight headaches. When Friday came, we arrived home from school early. None of us felt well. Since our headaches persisted, we went to bed early.

Sabbath, at 2:00 A.M., I awoke with a start. I heard someone being sick in the bathroom. I sat up. My head ached severely. I thought, *We must have caught a bad flu bug.* Drowsy, I moved toward the bathroom and pushed open the door to find my son, Jeremy, passed out on the floor!

"Jeremy! Jeremy! Wake up!" I snatched up a cloth, moistened it, and washed his face. He responded, and I helped him back to bed. The next morning, Jeremy and I both felt dizzy and nauseous. Daughter Stephanie picked at her breakfast, but insisted she felt well enough to walk to Sabbath School. After Sabbath School, she returned home and took a nap in the back bedroom. An hour later she awoke—disoriented and vomiting.

After church, friends stopped by and invited the children to their house for lunch. "This way you can get some rest," they told me, and I agreed. I strolled to the back bedroom and slept for two hours. Suddenly I was awakened by a hard blow to my chest. I saw no one in the room. My heart beat erratically. My strength slipped away, and I slid to the floor. I managed to crawl down the hallway. Halfway between the bedroom and the living room, I lost consciousness for several minutes. When I awoke, I struggled toward the phone. "I'm disoriented . . . I feel like I'm on my way out," I told my friend when he answered the phone.

"I'll be right over to get you!"

Within minutes, my friend burst through the door and rushed me to the hospital. The doctor's examination showed an irregular heartbeat, but no other problems. However, forty minutes after I entered the hospital, the blood drawn and tested revealed a high level of carbon monoxide.

"You are one fortunate man, Mr. Fritz," the doctor said. "Had you stayed in that house fifteen to twenty minutes longer, your family would be planning your funeral now."

When friends of the school maintenance department checked the furnace system in the house, they found the old furnace exhaust sealed and the new duct left open. Hence, the new furnace exhausted through the old exhaust system. While winterizing the house, I accidentally plugged the wrong exhaust pipe.

A series of providential circumstances saved our family from carbon monoxide poisoning. I shudder to think that if our youngest daughter had not gone with my wife and her parents to Minnesota, she likely would have taken a nap in the back bedroom situated directly over the furnace—and may not have ever awakened. Had friends not insisted on taking the two other children home for lunch after church, one or both could have succumbed. I'm sure my guardian angel beat my chest to awaken me and startled me with extreme, irregular heart beats. He also gave me the strength to get to the phone or I would have died from that invisible poison. Even though I caused this situation to develop, we had no idea at the time why we were developing these symptoms.

This experience proved to our family that God surely demonstrated His care and planned each circumstance in our lives to save our entire family. We are told in Matthew 6:25–27, " 'Do not worry about your life, what you will eat or drink; or about your body, what you will wear. . . . Who of you by worrying can add a single hour to his life?' " (NIV).

Even today, as I think of this experience, I thank God for His loving protection over our family during that cold Colorado winter and for the watchfulness of our guardian angels.

As told by Gottfried Fritz.

CHAPTER 17

Above Nushagak's Muddy Waters

Those whose radios were tuned to the proper ship-to-shore frequency in Alaska's Bristol Bay area one day during the summer of 1970 heard this call—"KXK 70. KXK 70. This is KWE 80 Ekuk. This is an emergency!"

It was the middle of the fishing season for the red salmon run. Along the Nushagak River many family camps were set up to catch the salmon as they made their way up river to their spawning beds. The families were using the set-net method, and when the run of fish hit the nets, it was a busy time for everyone. But between runs there was time for fun and play, especially for the young people.

On this particular day Brent Cummings, age eleven, had been having great sport with a mud sled. A mud sled is merely a piece of tin nailed to plywood to form a small flat-bottomed boat. These sleds are used to haul the fish ashore as the nets are emptied, but today Brent had an entirely different use for the one he had commandeered. In his lively imagination, this mud

sled had become a mighty gill-netting ship with no less a per-
sonage with Captain Brent Cummings in command. He was
having so much fun that he was completely unaware his "ship"
had increased its speed until he looked up to take his bearings
and saw he was rapidly moving into the faster current of the
river.

Having grown up in Alaska, Brent had developed the drive
and self-reliance of a typical Alaskan. Firmly he grasped the
only paddle he had aboard, a long stick, and muttered through
tight lips, "Put everything you've go into it if you ever hope to
get back to shore!" But the distance between himself and the
shoreline was widening every second. As he sized up the situation, his decision was quick: "My only chance is to swim it," he
decided.

Instantly, he plunged into the icy waters. Brent was a good
swimmer, but in his excitement he forgot that he was fully clothed
in rain gear and boots. He fought with every ounce of his strength
to stay afloat and get off his heavy clothing, but it was a losing
battle.

In one of the cabins along the beach, Brent's grandmother
stepped to the door and looked out toward the water at the
precise moment that Brent went over the side of the mud sled.
She saw him make his desperate effort to swim and then sink
from sight. She began screaming, "Brent! Brent's drowning. Help!
Help!"

A crowd, mostly children, quickly gathered. Among them
was Robin, Brent's cousin, who was fourteen years old. Instantly kicking off his boots and throwing aside his outer clothing, Robin dashed into the water and struck out for the area

where he had seen Brent's head for a fleeting second. There he began treading water, watching hopefully for another glimpse of Brent.

Because of the extreme muddiness of the water of the Bristol Bay area, it's impossible to see anything below its surface. Robin could only wait and watch as he prayed from the depths of his heart, "Oh, God, save him!"

Then it happened. Miracle of miracles, there was a bump against Robin's leg. It was Brent coming up once more at the very spot where Robin was treading water. In the last throes of drowning, he clutched his cousin wildly. Robin struggled desperately to break Brent's stranglehold; it seemed that both boys would surely go down together.

In the meantime, farther up the Nushagak, a workman straightened up from his activity to rest himself. His eyes casually followed the shoreline toward the mouth of the river. Suddenly the casualness ended.

"Something's wrong," he shouted, and jumping into his jeep, he sped to the scene of commotion, arriving in time to give a helping hand to Robin, who was near exhaustion from his heroic battle to save Brent. Dragging the unconscious boy to the shore, the workman and others tried frantically to restore Brent's breathing.

A short distance away was a cabin owned by Dr. Libby, a practicing physician in a town some twenty miles away. Just the day before, the doctor had been at his cabin. As he had sat by his radio making ship-to-shore contacts, one of Brent's aunts had been present. She had found herself taking an exceptionally keen interest in the operation of the radio. Now, as she looked down at her nephew so drastically in need of a doctor's skill, she exclaimed, "Dr. Libby's radio! I think I can manage to get a message out on it. At least I can try." And she was off like a flash.

Frantically someone called after her, "But you can't possibly get to the radio. The cabin is locked."

Under ordinary circumstances this would have been true, but somehow there had been an oversight, and the cabin door readily swung open.

With trembling fingers she began manipulating the radio just as she had observed Dr. Libby doing the day before. "Oh, heavenly Father," she implored, "help this call go out and be picked up by someone who will quickly relay it to the doctor's office."

Despite her anxiety, she spoke the words with deliberate clearness: "KXK 70. KXK 70. This is KWE 80 Ekuk. This is an emergency! The Cummings boy has drowned. Call Dr. Libby and have him fly to the fish camp immediately."

As efforts to revive Brent continued, the drone of an airplane was heard. "Could it be the doctor?"

Yes, Dr. Libby's seaplane was coming in for a landing. The message had gotten through! And because of all that had already been done, the doctor was able to bring Brent back to complete consciousness.

Brent quickly became the same healthy, energetic boy he had been when he had set forth on his imaginary gill-netting ship a short time earlier. Nor did his cousin Robin suffer any ill effects from his fierce struggle and narrow escape in the icy waters of the river.

But what might have been the story if Grandmother had not seen Brent dive from the mud sled? What if Robin had not been treading water at the precise location where Brent surfaced? What if the workman with the jeep had not noticed the commotion along the shore? What if the doctor's cabin door had been locked? What if Brent's aunt had not been capable of operating the radio or if the message had not been picked up and relayed to Dr. Libby?

The Nushagak River, undisturbed by the near double tragedy, continued its steady flow into Bristol Bay that day, but above its muddy waters were six undeniable evidences of God's providential love and care in the timely events that led to the saving of two brave Christian boys.

As written by Mabel Latsha.
First published by Guide, Volume 20, Number 4.
Used by permission.

CHAPTER 18

Over the Rails

The 1916 Model T Ford chugged merrily along the graveled country road, its brass radiator shining in the morning sun. It was headed toward the town of Glendive on the Yellowstone River in eastern Montana.

Marie and Claudette, the fifteen- and sixteen-year-old occupants of the Ford, were feeling lighthearted, for this day held promises of being exceptionally pleasant. Their older sister, Leona, a telegraph operator, would be coming into town that morning and leaving on the late afternoon train. This would give the three sisters several hours to be together—a privilege they felt came altogether too seldom.

As they were crossing the bridge that spanned the Yellowstone just before entering Glendive, loose planks rattled noisily beneath the wheels of the Ford. Marie shouted above the racket, "It surely will be a relief when the repair work is completed on this bridge!"

Soon Claudette, the older of the two, had parked the car on the main street of the business district, and the girls eagerly glanced about for a glimpse of Leona. There she stood waiting and watching for them in front of the Douglas and Meade department store.

Bubbly greetings were quickly exchanged, and the girls were off for a happy day of shopping and girl talk.

All too soon it was time to make their way to the railroad depot. As Leona boarded her train, she paused for one more farewell wave to Claudette and Marie. Standing on the station platform, the two girls felt a choked-up feeling in their throats as they stared after the big black cars gliding farther and farther down the shining rails.

Then Marie said with a start, "We can't just stand here. Let's go to the car." In their little Ford they headed toward the bridge and home where their mother would be waiting for them to give a full report of the day's visit with Leona.

But they soon learned it would be quite some time before they would be getting home. As they neared the approach to the bridge, a row of red lanterns hanging from a low frame blocked their way.

"What's this?" both girls exclaimed at the same time. Ahead on the bridge they could see workmen busy with crowbars, hammers, and other tools as old worn planks were being removed and new ones laid in their place. No traffic whatsoever was able to cross.

A groan escaped Claudette's lips as she pointed to a large sign which read simply, "Bridge closed for repairs between the hours of 6 P.M. and 6 A.M.

"Now why didn't we read that sign when we came into town this morning?" She scolded. "We're in a real predicament."

Marie's eyes were big and round, and her voice was full of concern as she asked, "Whatever are we to do? We've got to get home. Mother will be worried sick about us, and there's no way of getting word to her."

Claudette did not answer right away. She looked deeply troubled. Finally she tossed her head with determination and said, "We're walking. We'll park the car back in town and start walking."

"Oh, no!" Marie exclaimed with a shudder. "Four long miles—and it will soon be dark!"

"We have no other choice," Claudette reminded her.

After leaving their car, they took a shortcut through the railroad yard. Darkness was closing in on them, and they must not lose a moment. Over the tracks they ran, up and over the many rails. Finally they came to the main line. Only two more rails to cross. But a big round headlight glaring at them from up the track and the cry of the whistle warned them that a train was traveling on that main line.

"It might be a long freight train," Claudette panted. "We've got to be quick and get across ahead of it."

With the one thought in mind of reaching home as quickly as possible, they both darted forward in spite of the warning whistle and the clanging of the bell.

Marie made it safely across, but poor Claudette—tired and anxious as she was—stumbled and fell headlong between the two rails. There was no time for Marie to give her a helping hand for now the fast-moving train appeared only a few yards from her sister's prostrate form.

"Oh God, help us!" Marie pleaded in utter helplessness.

The mighty engine roared by with its long string of box cars trailing noisily behind—but Claudette was not beneath it! She scrambled to her feet beside Marie, unharmed! Severely shaken by the near tragedy and awed by the unbelievable escape, neither girl spoke a word. They could only clasp each other's hand, and turning toward the bridge, they pressed on in silence.

Arriving at the bridge, they threaded their way over the torn-up planking and through the groups of working men to the far end. Once they crossed the lighted bridge, the roadway ahead of them loomed dark and forbidding. They were in the country now with no street lights or even a lighted window to make their going easier.

"Claudette," Marie ventured to whisper, "it's terribly dark, isn't it? And such a long, long way for us to walk alone."

"No, not alone," Claudette offered. "After what just happened in the railroad yard, I feel God is surely watching over us. Maybe after this experience we'll remember to pay attention to signs and warnings."

The freshly graveled road made walking a grueling experience. It crunched loudly under their feet, yet the noise wasn't so loud that they couldn't hear another crunching sound a short way behind them. Turning quickly, they saw a shadowy form moving steadily toward them. They tried to scream, in hope of being heard by the workmen on the bridge, but their throats were paralyzed with fear.

Then as the shadowy form drew nearer, it proved to be only a large, friendly dog. In a gentle manner he walked directly up to the girls and quietly stood beside them.

Claudette was the first to regain her composure enough to

wonder out loud, "Whose dog can he be? There are no farm-houses near here."

"He could belong to one of the men working on the bridge," Marie suggested in a quavering voice.

"Then we should try to send him back." With that Claudette pointed back toward the bridge and commanded, "Go back, boy, go back."

But the dog did not go back. He waited patiently until the girls decided they should not spend precious time arguing with a dog. Besides, he quickly appealed to them as being exceptionally good company in their situation. It didn't seem nearly so dark and lonely with him trotting along by their side.

Onward they trudged. From sheer weariness their stride had slowed down after the first couple of miles; but as they neared the last hill between themselves and home, their energies seemed to revive, and they were again walking with lively steps. Cresting the hill, they could see below them the lighted windows of home. With a surge of joy they were ready to break into a run when they noticed Mother standing in the lighted doorway. They knew she was anxiously listening for the sound of a car motor or the sight of car lights steadily descending the winding road.

Through cupped hands the girls called out, "We're coming. We're all right." Then to help ease Mother's bewilderment over their voices coming to her through the darkness and no car in evidence, they began singing cheerily, "There's a light in the win-dow, there's a light in the window, there's a light in the window for me."

Soon they were in the house giving a detailed report of the happy hours spent with Leona, the closed bridge, the sign they had failed to read, and the shortcut through the railroad yards with its horrifying experience. At this point Claudette said earnestly, "I was sure it was the end for me! There wasn't possibly time enough to scramble to my feet and get off the track. I felt an overpowering impulse to make a quick roll, and the next thing I knew I was up over the rail just as the flashing wheels of the engine went by. I've been thinking about it all the way home, Mother, and I can see only one explanation—it had to be my guardian angel that helped me over that rail, for I couldn't have done it by myself."

With tears of deep gratitude Mother responded, "Surely God has given us proof of His loving kindness tonight."

Gently patting the dog's head that had followed them along the way, Marie added solemnly, "And couldn't it be possible that even this wonderful dog was a part of God's kindness too?"

Claudette nodded in agreement as she too gave him a pat.

As written by Mabel Latsha.
First published in Guide, *Volume 19, Number 20.*
Used by permission.

CHAPTER 19

The Biggest German Shepherd

"I can hardly wait 'til tomorrow!" Lila, my ten-year-old, enthusiastically hopped from one foot to the other.

"Why? What's happening tomorrow?" I asked.

Lila stopped hopping and looked me squarely in the eye, "Mom, you haven't forgotten already, have you? Tomorrow our Pathfinder club marches in the Water Follies parade!" she said all in a single breath.

"Oh yes, I remember. You've told me that a dozen times now," I teased.

Our family lived in Rutland, a suburb of Kelowna, British Columbia, Canada, where my husband worked as the school principal. Every summer the Kelowna Aquatic Club planned the city's annual Water Follies. This year the Aquatic Club had invited Lila's Pathfinder club to march in the downtown parade. This was a "first" for their active club.

The next morning Lila went to town early with another family to get ready for the parade, while I tended the three younger children at home and packed a picnic lunch. I would drive to town later to watch the parade.

After the parade and a tasty picnic lunch in the park, I packed the leftovers and called to the romping children, "Time to get into the car and head for home!"

"Do we have to go already, Mom?" Lila frowned. "May I stay and come home with the Smiths?"

"OK. Do you know where to find them?" I asked.

"Yes! Over there." Lila pointed and ran their direction. The Pathfinder leaders had more club activities planned for the children in the park that afternoon, and Lila didn't want to miss the fun. I hustled the younger children into the car and drove home, confident that Lila would come later with the family who had taken her to town that morning.

At four o'clock I looked at the clock and wondered why Lila wasn't home yet. At five o'clock I wasn't wondering; I was worried! I called several club members' mothers to see if Lila had come home with them. All of them said, "I didn't see Lila anywhere!"

At 5:30 P.M. I put the children in the car and drove back to town. Praying, I arrived at the wide main street. I drove very slowly, while four pairs of eyes intently searched both sides of the street for a girl in a brown Pathfinder uniform. "I can't see her anywhere! Can you, children?"

"No!" they chorused. We couldn't find Lila anywhere along Main Street. At the park, still crowded with people, we all saw her at once! I made a quick U-turn and stopped. We all laughed, relieved that we'd found Lila so quickly. She was seated on the curb, but she wasn't alone. Beside her, yet somewhat behind her, was one of the biggest German shepherd dogs we'd ever seen! As we approached, he didn't make a friendly or unfriendly move. He just sat there quietly watching us.

"Where did he come from?" I asked, pointing to the dog.

"He came and sat beside me about two hours ago," Lila said.

After Lila joined us in the car, I bowed my head to thank God for protecting Lila. God knew Lila loved dogs and wouldn't be afraid of the mammoth-sized German shepherd.

As we drove away, we looked to see if the dog was still where we'd left him. He was nowhere in sight! We don't know if her guardian angel took on the form of a canine friend or whether the dog was sent by Lila's guardian angel to protect her from harm. It doesn't really matter. We are all convinced that God sent the biggest German shepherd ever to guard Lila after she'd missed her ride home. Hasn't our heavenly Father promised that "he shall give his angels charge over thee, to keep thee in all thy ways" (Psalm 91:11, KJV)?

As told by Grace Streifling.

CHAPTER 20

Taught by a Child

Children are beautiful in many ways. Children have taught me wonderful things; they are open-faced—quick to love, to trust, and to forgive. They are always full of wonder and excitement. Whether in sorrow or joy, children readily turn to Jesus, which is an inspiration for all of us.

Thinking of children and what we can learn from them, I think about an occasion that's embarrassing for me to tell. Actually, it is more than embarrassing; it's sort of shameful.

I have a habit I inherited. At least I like to say I inherited this habit because I don't want to take credit for it all by myself. The habit I inherited is to see how far I can get on a tank of gas even when the gauge crowds empty! I call it veggie-gambling. It just gives a little more thrill to life to think that you might run out of gas somewhere between Salt Lake and Cheyenne. Although my wife tries to keep gas in the car against my wishes, we sometimes run out of gas on our trips.

My children were preschoolers, and our family was driving

somewhere in our car. As we drove along, the car began to cough and sputter. It stalled, but I coasted to a stop beside the road. I looked at the gas gauge. Sure enough, we had run out of gas. We were still several miles from the next town. Personally, I don't mind running out of gas when I'm alone. But when my family is with me, it's a reminder of how I shouldn't be playing this game. My family is always sure to let me know that it is not a game they like to play.

"We never asked to play this game with you!" they'll say. "It's fine and good if you want to be a martyr, but remember that the real martyrs didn't take their families with them to the stake!"

Frustrated to have run out of gas when my family was with me, I hit the steering wheel. "Ah! Out of gas!" I exclaimed.

Lindsey, my little daughter, piped up from the back seat, "Daddy, let's just pray about it. Let's ask Jesus to help the car run. He'll get us to a station!"

I thought, *Oh come on, Lindsey, if Jesus planned to help us, He would have had to do it before now. The reason we're here beside the road is because we're out of gas and the car stopped running!*

"I think we ought to pray!" came the persistent voice behind me. "Let's pray and ask Jesus to help us!"

So what choice did I have? What else could I do? We had to pray. I thought, *This is surely putting You in a jam, Lord!* But I prayed to the One who told Moses to hit a rock, and enough water gushed out for three million people. I prayed, "Lord, You know, Lindsey told us to pray. Here we are beside the road out of gas. Would You help this car to start so we can get to a station, *please?*" I said, "Amen," turned on the ignition, and the car started! We drove to the next town, where we found gas!

Children don't hesitate to go to Jesus. Their simple prayers and confiding faith leave me envious. Is it any wonder that Jesus said, "Except ye . . . become as little children, ye shall not enter into the kingdom of heaven" (Matthew 18:3, KJV)? We can learn a lot from kids. They have an unwavering faith!

Children have a positive influence on us, but grown-ups can also have a good influence on children. If we are daily surrendered to God and are seeking to know Him better, then we can be used by heaven, in teamwork with angels, to point children to Jesus and lead them to Him. May the implicit faith of children become ours each day!

As told by Pastor Lee Venden.

CHAPTER 21

The Frozen Path

In 1914, my parents filed for a homestead in the flat prairie land about thirty miles from Glendive, Montana. In those horse-and-buggy days, it took us at least two days when we went to town to do our business and shopping—most of one day to drive to town and most of the second day to drive home. However, we had a post office and a small grocery store about ten miles away. We didn't go often for our mail. Many times, neighbors would go to the post office and pick up everyone's mail. They would pass the mail on to their neighbor, who in turn passed it on to their nearest neighbor until all the mail was delivered. No one had telephones in those days.

School was a one-room country schoolhouse. Our teacher was fresh out of teacher's training—a city girl from Minneapolis. She taught five grades to eight children—including me and my three sisters. We walked to school through the pastures. Due to the frigid winter blizzards, we missed many days of class. When weather improved, we trudged through deep snow to attend school. We loved our teacher and thought she was wonderful!

During winter, one to two feet of snow usually covered the countryside. On our way to school we made a path, packing the snow firmly as we walked through the open pasture. Soon the path built into a solid mass of ice. There was nothing to guide us, but we were hardy country girls and could take it. When March came, the snow would sometimes melt and leave patches of bare ground here and there. The snow always melted around our frozen path first, but the path itself remained to the last before disappearing.

One particular March morning we awoke to a balmy, sunny day. We were thrilled, because ordinarily March was chilly. Quickly, we did our chores. My older sister, Katherine, who was fifteen, milked the cows while we younger girls fed the chickens and gathered the eggs.

Jessica, just thirteen, was a feisty young lady. She asked, "Mom, we don't have to wear our heavy coats to school today, do we? It's so lovely and sunny out!"

Mother, who was ill in bed at the time, said, "Oh yes, girls, you must put on your regular winter wear because you don't know what the weather might be like this afternoon. Jessica, you and Mabel are invited to spend the night with your friend, Glenna, remember? You won't be coming home tonight, and tomorrow morning it may be much colder than this morning. You must put on your warm coats!"

We all obeyed and put on our heavy coats, but we didn't button them. And we didn't wrap our scarves around our necks as tightly as we usually did. The bright sun convinced us that spring had sprung. We were gloriously happy as we raced off to school along our frozen pasture path.

When first recess came, we were delighted not having to bundle up to play outdoors. How we all looked forward to the noon hour when we'd have more time to play outside in the sun!

Noon, however, brought a decided change in the weather. In the west we saw dark-blue, billowy clouds churning toward us. The air grew chilly. Disappointed in the sudden weather change, we went into the school to eat our lunches and begin our afternoon classes. While in class we looked out the window and saw little snowflakes falling. Soon a strong wind swirled the snowflakes into circles. We couldn't believe what we saw. Our beautiful morning was spoiled and gone! It kept on snowing and blowing. When afternoon recess arrived, our teacher became worried because of the increased snowfall and the strong wind that was blowing.

She told Katherine, my oldest sister, "Step outdoors with me for a minute. Let's check the weather. Maybe we should dismiss school early."

Once outdoors they found the weather worsening by the minute. "I can make it home all right," Katherine said. "I must start home at once because Mother is sick in bed, and she will be terribly worried if I don't show up."

"Are you sure you can make it OK?" our teacher asked, because she was new to the area and didn't understand the viciousness of our blizzards.

"If I start home right now, with the wind at my back and the frozen path to follow, I'll make it all right," Katherine reassured her.

"If you must go, Katherine, I'll dismiss school now for your sake."

While Katherine bundled up, her friend, Mildred, said, "I'm going with Katherine!" She also dressed in her warm clothes. Mildred lived just beyond our home.

Next Mildred's cousin, Vernon, a third-grader, spoke up, "I want to go with those girls, too." He dashed for his warm coat, and our teacher tucked in his scarf while he pulled on his mittens.

After the three children were dressed to face the storm, Katherine told our teacher, "We'll just go as far as the schoolyard gate. If we think it's too dangerous to go any farther, we'll come back."

By now our teacher felt quite anxious about this whole situation. She was responsible for the children's safety. She waited, thinking the three children would return in just a few moments. But they didn't return. "Since Katherine didn't come back, maybe the rest of us ought to try to make it home too," our teacher said. "If we stay here we will be without food or beds. If this storm should last a long time, we'd be in a bad way."

So the rest of us bundled ourselves into our wraps and stepped out into the storm with our teacher. We faced the wind. Since Jessica and I were going to spend the night at our friend's home, about two city blocks away, we—and all the rest of the group— went the opposite direction from the way Katherine and her two companions had gone. Soft, blowing snow blinded us.

"Walk single file and hang on to the coat of the person in front of you," our teacher told us. We braced ourselves against the wind and snow. There was a fence we could have followed, but it would be tough to try to keep in touch with the fence as well as with the person in front of us. We struggled trying to hold on to each other—sometimes stumbling and sometimes fall-ing. We didn't even get out of the schoolyard.

Finally our teacher said, "Children, let's turn around and go back to the schoolhouse. It's no use trying to fight this blizzard!" Back inside the school, she became more and more concerned about Katherine, Mildred, and Vernon. Would those three chil-dren make it across the prairie all right in this frightful storm? It was over a half mile to our home from school, but Katherine had promised she would keep her eyes on the frozen path. We were glad that it was still daylight.

Our teacher knew that Jessica and I came from a praying fam-ily. As she became more and more worried, she quietly asked the two of us to pray. "Pray as you've never prayed before," she whis-pered, not wanting to alarm the other children. We prayed si-lently and earnestly that Katherine and her two friends would get to our home safely and that someone would come to our rescue at school.

Meanwhile Katherine had remembered her promise that when she got to the school gate she would return if the storm got worse. But when they arrived at the gate and turned to go back, they couldn't see the school for the storm!

"I can't see the school, but I can still see the frozen path," Katherine told her friends. "So let's follow this frozen path, and I'm sure we'll make it OK. Let's stay close together." Each clung to the coat of the one in front as Katherine led them along the frozen path. They stumbled, moving slowly on the path; it was their only hope of finding home in the blinding snowstorm.

Finally, they arrived at a shack that stood less than a quarter mile from Katherine's home. They were too numb and cold to continue, so Katherine led the children to the door. She raised her frozen hand to knock on the door as loudly as she could. No one answered. Desperately she tried to turn the doorknob with her numb hand, but found it tightly locked!

"Now, whatever shall we do, Katherine?" Mildred asked.

"I'm half frozen already!"

"Let's go to the barn," Katherine grabbed Vernon's hand. They faced the wind and struggled toward the dug-out barn near the shack. They opened the door. All they found was an empty barn—no hay, no straw or horse blankets! But at least they were now out of the ferocious wind and the pelting snow. They stomped back and forth cross the length of the barn, trying to get their circulation back and their feet warm. They swung their arms and clapped their hands until they began feeling circulation once again.

When their feet and hands felt somewhat warmer, Katherine faced her companions and said, "We can't stay here in the barn all night. If we do, we'll freeze to death before morning." She was right; it was bitterly cold. "We have to face the storm again," she continued. "We have to try to find the frozen path and keep on going home." The other two were heartsick!

"Whatever you say, Katherine," Mildred wearily replied.

"Before we step out into the storm again, we've got to pray," Katherine suggested. The children with her didn't come from praying homes, but they knew there was a God.

"Dear Lord," Katherine prayed sincerely, "please help us find the frozen path and send Your angels to guide us safely home."

Back out in the storm, they were able to find the frozen path in spite of the wind and snow. But they also realized that it was dusk and would soon be dark. Katherine, in the lead, kept wiggling her feet, feeling for the rough, frozen path. That made slow going, but the little group kept moving. Finally they stumbled into the garden fence of home. Encouraged, they knew they were only a little ways from the house. They had to follow the garden fence a short distance, turn, go a little farther, and make another turn which would bring them to the gate and pathway that would lead them to the door.

Sick as she was, Mother was frantic with worry. She wanted to go look for her girls. But Dad tried to assure her that the teacher would never allow the children to leave school in such a storm. As time passed, Mother insisted. She began putting on her heavy winter coat, and Dad hastily began doing the same. He wasn't going to allow Mother go out in that storm alone even though he knew it might mean the end for both of them. Just before they went outside, they heard voices calling, "Open the door!"

Once inside, the children couldn't remove their jackets because the snow had frozen them against their chests. Dad took a knife and chipped away at the snow on their jackets so that they could finally unbutton and remove them. Then he treated the children's hands and feet for frostbite.

Those of us at school kept warm because we had plenty of coal to keep the fire going. The teacher did her best to keep us calm. She read stories to us. We sang and played games. We were hungry, but no one felt sleepy. I was extremely worried that my older sister, Katherine, had died out in the storm. I remember thinking, *How are we ever going to live without Katherine?*

About midnight the wind died down, and things became very quiet. We couldn't believe it! The storm that had come so sud-

denly, left just as abruptly. Soon after it became calm, we heard
footsteps on the snow. Mr. Stiemann, the father of the home
where Jessica and I were to have spent the night, opened the door.
He quickly glanced around the room, saw the children there, and
said, "Thank God! You're all safe!"

"No! No!" our anxious teacher exclaimed. "Katherine,
Mildred, and Vernon are out there somewhere!"

"Don't you worry!" Mr. Stiemann said, "Katherine is a level-
headed girl. If she thought they could make it home, they made
it home." Those words encouraged everyone. He'd brought a big
basket of sandwiches and passed them to us hungry children.
Those sandwiches tasted most delicious! When we finished eating, we bundled up, and he led us all to his home. There we sat
down to bowls of hot soup.

Jessica and I were still worried about Katherine. We went to
bed, but it took us hours to get to sleep. I kept wondering, *How
are we ever going to live without Katherine!*

When morning came, Vernon's father came directly to the
Stiemann home looking for his son. He said, "I figured the children would still all be at school. Where is Vernon?"

"Vernon left school with Katherine yesterday afternoon!" Mr.
Stiemann told him. He immediately left for our home and found
that Katherine, Mildred, and Vernon had arrived at our house
safely. He told our parents that Jessica and I were also safe.

I have not the slightest doubt that, in answer to many, many
prayers, angels were sent to guide Katherine's frigid feet along the
frozen path to our garden fence and finally home safely!

As told by Mabel Latsha.

CHAPTER 22

Before They Call

My faith has been tried many times. Often I've knelt, asking God for wisdom and direction during trying circumstances. Sometimes, God has intervened even before I asked Him!

An elderly friend called me one Sunday morning and asked, "Barbara, could you please take my sister-in-law to the airport? Her plane leaves at ten, and my grandson is unable to take us."

"I'd be more than glad to," I answered. I drove to my friend's home, loaded the luggage, helped the ladies into the car, and started for the airport. Before we got halfway there, steam gushed out from under the hood of my car. I looked at the panel where the temperature gauge was flashing red. *Oh no!* I thought. *What am I going to do?*

I had just gotten onto the freeway and was still about four and a half miles from the airport. I decided to keep driving slowly even though we felt the car interior grow hotter and hotter. "Lord, help me!" I whispered. We made it to the airport. We unloaded the luggage and carried it to the ticket desk.

After my car cooled, I told my friend, "You stay here and see your sister-in-law off, while I go find a gas station and see what's the matter with my car."

As I turned to go, the sister-in-law pushed some money into my hand. "Take this!" she said.

"Oh no! You don't need to do this. I'm more than glad to help," I insisted.

"You keep it! I would have paid this much for a taxi."

I didn't want to argue with her, so I thanked her and shoved the bill deep into my pocket without looking at it.

"I'll be right back," I told them and hurried toward my car. At first, it seemed to run all right, but before I got back to town, steam billowed again from under the hood. The first gas station I found was closed. I crept to the center of town before I found an open station.

Approaching two workmen, I said, "I'm not sure what's happening to my car. My radiator may only need water. Please look at it." They carefully lifted the hood and kept trying to remove the hot radiator cap as steam sizzled and sputtered!

"Stand back!" one man cautioned. "If steam starts to blow, you could get burned." I felt concerned for their safety. Finally the radiator cooled. The service man looked inside and found there was plenty of water in the radiator—so that wasn't the problem. After further checking, he discovered that the thermostat wasn't working to trigger the fan into cooling the radiator. He had to replace the thermostat.

I really don't have the money to pay for this! I thought to myself. *What am I going to do?* I reached into my pocket and discovered the lady had given me a twenty dollar bill. Shoving the bill back into my pocket, I hoped it would cover the repair cost. I kept thinking, *How am I going to get my friend from the airport?* I asked the service man, "May I use your phone?"

"Yes, go right ahead," he said. I called several people to ask if they could pick up my friend from the airport, but no one could.

The repairman overheard my calls and understood that no one could help me. He said, "This repair job will take a while, so take our company truck and get the lady. Take her home. By the time you get back, we should have your car ready."

"Are you going to charge me for the use of your truck?"

"Oh no! Go ahead and take it. You've got a situation here that needs help."

"Thank you so much!"

When I returned to the station, the service man greeted me, "Your car is ready for you. We replaced the thermostat, emptied the radiator, and put in fresh water and new antifreeze.

"I didn't authorize you to do all that!" I said. "How much is this going to cost?"

"I'll just charge you twenty dollars. It really would cost you more for my labor, but I'll charge you just twenty dollars."

Lord, I breathed a silent prayer, *You knew just how much this was going to cost! Before I even asked, You knew this was going to happen and provided the necessary money! Thank You!*

I gave the man the twenty dollar bill and thanked him saying, "Do you know, I didn't have the money for this repair job, but the woman I took to the airport gave it to me—just enough to cover your charge!"

"I was having a bad day," he replied, "until you came, and I saw your day was even worse than mine. So I thought I'd do a kind deed today."

"Thank you, so much! I don't know if you're religious or not, but the Lord has certainly blessed me by providing twenty dollars and for your help. I'm going to pray that God will bless you for your kindness."

I drove from the station praising the Lord because He'd supplied my needs even before I called on Him. I thought of the Bible promise, "Before they call, I will answer; and while they are yet speaking, I will hear" (Isaiah 65:24, KJV).

As told by Barbara Dunston-LaRose.
First published in Adventist Review, May 29, 2003.
Used by permission.

CHAPTER 23

Transported by an Angel

It appeared that my life's destiny was to become a pastor. Even during my academy years in Indiana I was asked to preach at several churches. After graduation at the age of eighteen, I received an invitation to pastor the Bedford, Indiana, church, which had no regular pastor at the time. Readily I accepted the invitation to spend one year as the Bedford pastor before going on to college. My decision came easily because I was already well acquainted with several of the members there.

Near the close of that year, my uncle in Colorado suggested that I spend some time with his family before enrolling in college. That appealed to me. I felt the need for relaxation and a little youthful adventure. However, I had very little money—and no car. The compensation from the church was limited because I was not on a regular salary. I decided to travel to Colorado OPC (other people's cars), also known as hitchhiking.

Shortly after reaching the highway, I began making the customary thumb signal to passing motorists. Soon a gentleman stopped and asked, "Where are you headed, young man?"

"La Junta, Colorado," I replied.

"Jump in," he said. "I can take you as far as St. Louis." I sat down in the seat beside him. The ride was enjoyable, and our visit pleasant.

When we arrived in the heart of St. Louis, near his destination, he said, "Here we are, young man! I will let you out just across the Mississippi River."

As I opened the car door to leave, I said, "Thanks for the enjoyable ride and visit!" He smiled and waved. I walked into the night.

Even though I was unacquainted with the area, I knew I should get on a street going west before I began to thumb for another ride. Apparently my choice of streets was unwise. Within a matter of minutes, I felt a tap on my shoulder and looked up into the face of a tall police officer.

"Where are you going?" he asked.

"Eventually, I plan to reach my uncle's home in La Junta, Colorado! My uncle invited me to come visit his family."

He placed his hand on my shoulder and said kindly, "Son, you're in a very dangerous area at this time of night. Let me help you get to a safe place." He picked up my heavy suitcase and started walking. I followed. It seemed but just a few minutes until we came to a well-lit street. There he pointed to a motel located on the highway which I would need to take out of town.

"At that motel you'll find reasonable facilities for the night," he advised. I turned my gaze from the motel to thank him for his help, but he was gone! I looked for a side street down which he might have turned—but there was none anywhere. I looked up and down the street I was standing in—but couldn't see him. He'd absolutely vanished!

At the motel I found a reasonable room, studied my Bible lesson, and went to bed. The following morning, a lovely young couple picked me up and took me almost to Colorado! At the time, I didn't really realize what had happened the night before.

Later when I became better acquainted with the city of St. Louis, I realized that, in reality, it would have taken several hours to walk from the downtown area where the gentleman had first let me out of his car to the far western side of the city where the motel was located. That kind policeman had to be none other than my guardian angel! He had transported me almost instantly from the dangerous downtown area of the city to the west side, where he pointed out the motel and vanished. I'm convinced that my heavenly Father sent His protecting angel in the form of a policeman to save me from danger.

Thank God for protecting—and transporting—guardian angels!

As told by Paul T. Jackson.

CHAPTER 24

The Giant Hero

Nearing his destination, Don noticed his gas gauge nearing "empty." "Oh, no!" he exclaimed, "I thought I could make it into town on the gas I had!" Soon his loaded semi lumbered to a stop. There weren't even enough gas fumes left to coast another inch! Don clambered out of the cab and hiked about a mile to the nearest phone to call his wife.

"Sara, you won't believe this, but I ran out of gas about ten miles northeast of Vancouver! Do you think you could bring me a few gallons so that I could at least make it into town and a gas station?" Don gave Sara specific directions to his location.

"It may take me thirty minutes or longer to get the gas and find you," Sara warned him.

"That's OK, I won't be going anywhere!"

As dusk edged out the daylight, Sara found Don and handed him the gas she'd brought. He poured it into the truck's tank and climbed behind the steering wheel. Sara drove the family car ahead of Don's truck as they headed toward town. Suddenly a car rounded a curve and met Sara head on, forcing her off the right side of the road. At the same time, Don swerved into the left lane to avoid a collision. His truck hit the soft shoulder and rolled. Fortunately, it landed right-side-up!

Sara flagged down a passing motorist, "Call the sheriff's office!" she screamed. "My husband is in that flaming truck over the bank!" She pointed to the crashed truck.

The motorist nodded and raced for help. Soon several police officers and a wrecker congregated. Quickly, they extinguished the blaze. But they couldn't open the crushed door to the cab— even with cables and using the Jaws of Life.

"Get the cutting torches ready!" one officer shouted.

Just then out of the night, a giant Black man strode up to the group. At a glance, he saw Don trapped in the cab of his still smoldering truck. "Can I help?" he asked.

"Sure, give it a try!" the sheriff told the huge, muscular man, as the others all backed away.

The stranger climbed up to the cab, placed his hands on the door, and wrenched it from its hinges. Climbing into the cab, he planted his feet on the floor and pushed his neck and shoulders against the top of the cab. The metal creaked as it gave way. The cab's top bowed upward. The seat settled downward. The dash broke under the giant's unbelievable strength!

"I saw that man's shirt sleeves rip as his muscles bulged," the officer reported later. Don fell free into the waiting arms of astonished deputy sheriffs. In the excitement of rescuing the unconscious driver, no one thought to thank the giant hero. He strode off into the night and vanished as quietly as he'd appeared.

"No one got his name," the deputy sheriff said later of the giant rescuer, "but he did the job I couldn't do with six men and a wrecker. It was a terrific display of human strength!"

Was it really a display of human strength? Was it a super-human adrenalin flush? Or could the man have been endowed with divine strength in a dire situation? Perhaps the giant hero wasn't human at all! Don and Sara believe that God sent His strongest angel to rescue Don that dark night.

CHAPTER 25

His Angels Kept Us

We had spent a restful week on the Oregon coast. Reluctantly, we decided it was time to end our vacation and head home to California. After my husband, Oscar, and I talked things over, we decided to spend the weekend in Eugene, Oregon, not far away. That way we would have a better start down I-5 and would have to spend only one night driving in the hot weather near Coaling before getting home.

We like to travel an hour or more before breakfast, so we arose early Thursday morning to begin our journey to Eugene. This time we decided not to tow the car, because we would need it in Eugene to attend church. I drove our car to the entrance of the RV park where we had been staying and waited for Oscar to follow with our motor home. Finally I saw him walking toward the car.

"The RV has no headlights," he said. "Do we stay here in Florence and try to get them fixed? Or shall we wait until daylight and go to Eugene and have them fixed there?"

We decided to go to the larger city of Eugene to take care of our headlight problem. When we arrived in Eugene, we immediately began calling every electrical company listed in the RV books. One fixed only trucks. Another did not fix headlights. Two companies didn't have time to work on our RV because they were booked for two weeks ahead already. I picked up the phone to make one last call.

"Sir, we have a thirty-foot RV. Our headlights aren't working. Can you help us?"

"Yes, I can!" came the welcome reply.

Friday morning at 8:00 the mechanic, Jim, began working on our RV. He worked all morning. We could only imagine what it would cost!

"I'll fix it so you will never have any more trouble," Jim reassured us. "Your original wiring isn't sufficient to carry your electrical load." When we came into the office to pay the bill, we found it was much less than we had anticipated.

"You know," Oscar told Jim, "I think it was almost providential that we found you to fix our problem."

Jim looked at Oscar and replied, "No, it was not 'almost' providential. It *was* providential! I saw you had your Bible on the front seat." He paused and continued, "You see, I had an RV just like yours. I bought it secondhand, and my lights went out while driving in the middle of the night when I was going around a curve. When your wife said you had no lights, I knew exactly what was wrong. The manufacturer doesn't put in heavy enough wiring or the proper connector. You could have easily had a fire."

He showed us the melted part and wiring; "My vehicle had been in a fire," Jim continued. "The repairman put the same inefficient connector back on it. That would have happened to you, too, if you had gone to anyone else for repairs. God took care of me, too," he added, "when my lights went out!"

We thanked Jim and paid him. We also thanked the Lord for His guidance to Jim's repair shop that day!

As told by Oralee Teske.

CHAPTER 26

The Lord Guides Continually

In the early 1950s we lived in Winnipeg, Manitoba, Canada. There my husband was the pastor of the Ukrainian Church. One young family, with five precious children, was having problems that were getting worse and worse instead of better.

Early one morning I was impressed to telephone the family to see how things were going. But because it was the time of morning that the mother would be busy feeding her children and getting them ready for school, I decided to wait. I promised myself I would call later—after the children had gone to school. But the impression came again and again: "Call Helen! Call Helen, now!"

Finally, I yielded to the persistent impression and called. "Have your children gone to school already?" I asked.

"Yes, they just left," she said. "How did you know to phone me? I had just picked up a knife to end my life, when the phone rang. How did you know to call me?"

"The Lord impressed me to call you, Helen!" I replied. "Please put down the knife and tell me what the trouble is."

My husband, who was nearby, heard my end of the conversation and realized there was trouble. He whispered to me, "Keep her talking on the phone until you know that I'm there." He dashed out the door, quickly picked up a nearby church deacon, and made a flying trip to Helen's home. In spite of being stopped for speeding and getting a ticket, he was able to get there in time to save Helen's life.

I managed to keep her talking on the phone by reciting Bible promises. Those promises came to my mind freely—just as though I were reading them to her from the Bible.

My husband and the deacon spent most of the day at Helen's home. In prayer, they asked God to help her. They implored God to send His angels to watch over her. The Lord heard their prayers and helped her. Even today we praise His name for answering our prayers in Helen's behalf. We thank our heavenly Father for watching over her during the most difficult time in her life. Helen is still alive and well—serving the Lord!

Truly, the Lord guided me to follow that strong impression the morning Helen planned to end her life. We're promised that "The LORD shall guide thee continually, and satisfy thy soul in drought, and make fat thy bones: and thou shalt be like a watered garden, and like a spring of water, whose waters fail not" (Isaiah 58:11, KJV).

As told by Anne Samograd.

CHAPTER 27

Lad on a Bicycle

One calm winter evening, I said to my wife, "Let's visit our neighbors this evening. What do you say?"

"I guess that might be a nice thing to do. We haven't visited with them in a while." We donned our warm coats and drove our four-wheel-drive truck into our neighbor's yard. After we visited with them for a couple of hours, we decided to return home. When we stepped out of their house, we noticed that the weather had turned cold with a blustery wind.

The roads were somewhat icy, and when we came to a sharp turn, we skidded. The front wheels landed in the bank beside the road. I crawled out of the truck to see what I could do to get out of the snow bank and decided it would be impossible to get out of that predicament. *What shall I do now?* I pondered. It was extremely cold, and I wasn't dressed warmly enough to walk to a farmer's home to obtain help.

I placed my arm on the fender of my truck, put my head on my arm, and prayed, "Dear Lord, You see the situation we're in! Please send someone to help us! Amen."

Just as I reached to open the door of the truck, I looked to one side. There I saw a young lad peddling his bicycle toward me! He stopped. It shocked me to see him dressed only in a shirt without a cap or jacket.

"Mister, are you having trouble?" he asked.

"Not really," I replied, "but I don't know how to put this truck into four-wheel drive."

"It's easy, no problem!" he said. "You want me to try it for you?"

"Yes! Please try," I told him. Immediately he jumped into the truck. With ease he shoved the gears into four-wheel drive, and then backed the truck out of the snow drift and onto the road.

After he slid out of the truck and I was about to climb in, my wife suggested, "Put his bicycle in the back of the truck and let's take him home." I turned to suggest this idea to the young lad, but there was no one there. I walked around the truck looking for him, but there was no trace of him or his bicycle!

Right then and there I bowed my head and thanked God for answering my prayer so promptly and sending a guardian angel in the form of a lad on a bicycle.

As told by Paul Hyrhirchuk.

CHAPTER 28

Angel Deliverance

After Raymond and I were married during the mid sixties, we lived in Glendale, California. Raymond worked for a company in Los Angeles that made special plastic covers for the nose of each jet plane. He supervised a group of men for the company. Raymond enjoyed his work even though he occasionally had to work overtime.

Raymond liked nature—especially tropical fish. He was the president of the local California Tropical Fish Club. As president, he would help the club members collect door prizes or trophies from various pet shops or tropical fish dealers, which they gave to people who attended their club meetings. These dealers eagerly donated fish food and beautiful, colorful fish. Occasionally a shop owner even donated a ten-gallon fish tank to be given as a door prize. But usually the prizes consisted of tiny blue, green, red, or black tropical fish.

One summer Saturday evening Raymond was scheduled to speak at the club meeting in Simi Valley. He also was to bring all of the door prizes to be given away that evening. After sundown, Raymond packed his car with the donated prizes. We got into our car and started climbing higher and higher through a mountain range with steep cliffs on one side of the highway. Traffic was light, so our trip seemed pleasant.

All of a sudden, Raymond heard a commanding voice speak to him, "Ray, pull off the road!" Raymond immediately pulled off the road, and the loud voice spoke to him again, "STOP!" Raymond stopped at once! Seconds later, a speeding car raced down the mountain toward us on our side of the road—the "wrong" side of the road for him. Had Raymond not heeded the speaking voice, pulling off the road as quickly as he did, we would have been victims of a head-on collision! In seconds there would not have been anything left of our car or us.

We don't know whether the speeding driver was drunk, on drugs, or if his car just went out of control due to the loss of brakes or some other mechanical failure. But we do know that our guardian angel protected us and saved our lives from a tragic accident. How thankful we are to our guardian angel for quickly directing Raymond to the side of the road. Thank God for our guardian angels!

As told by Helen Hyrchuk-Bishop.

CHAPTER 29

In Cooperation With an Angel

After our plane arrived in Seoul, South Korea, I walked down the jetway, relieved to be safely on the ground. I had shocked myself by my decision to leave the comforts of home and venture nearly halfway around the world to teach English at the In'Chon Language Institute. I'd never been a traveler. When I was only six years old, my parents and grandparents would go sightseeing on the Alaskan Bay. But I preferred my favorite spot—curled up in my bed reading Uncle Arthur's *Bedtime Stories.* Others of my family traveled to Europe or other faraway places. Part of me might wish I were going too, but I seldom went anywhere. I was content to stay near home.

I chose to go to Korea to make a change in my life from nursing. I had decided to broaden my life's experiences, so in 1989 I applied for service, filling out forms for both the U.S. Army and the Adventist Mission Service. If nothing materialized from these applications, I planned to write to the Peace Corps. The Adventist Mission Service replied, suggesting volunteer service in Korea. As my plans materialized, I became excited about teaching English in Korea. That would be a nice change from my nursing career.

Once I arrived in Korea, in 1990, I seldom ventured even to the post office by myself. Twice when I attempted to go for a walk alone, I got lost for three hours. After that I decided never to go anywhere alone. One day I discovered my shoes needed repairing. I was afraid to go across the street to the shoe repair shop by myself. Another teacher consented to take the shoes to the repair shop for me. However, I had to go and get the shoes myself. A natural adventurer, I certainly was not!

Despite all my nonadventuring spirit, I did go many places during my years in Korea. The school took trips, and the students eagerly showed me the historical sites of In'Chon and Seoul. We visited the waterfront and watched huge ships come into port. In Seoul, we visited the palace museums. We traveled to see rivers; we crossed lakes and climbed mountains. We visited temples and churches in many provinces, but during my early days in Korea, I never ventured on trips alone.

One week, feeling homesick, I came across Isaiah 54:1. "For more are the children of the desolate than the children of the married wife, saith the LORD" (KJV). I shared this text with one of my Bible classes. From that day onward, most of my students called me "Mom"!

One day a student approached me and said, "Mom . . . ?" He paused and urgently repeated, "Mom?"

"What is it?" I asked.

"Mom, you must really pray hard for this school. There is trouble here right now!" That's all he would tell me.

Later, after two of the strongest and most influential young teachers left to continue their education, the school seemed vacant and even stagnant.

Although I wasn't aware of any specific trouble, I walked outdoors and prayed. It was a serious time of prayer. I did what I knew how to do best—I cleaned and prayed, pulled weeds and prayed, mulched the garden and bushes around the building, continually praying. For about a month, between classes, I scrubbed and prayed for our school.

One morning, as I descended the marble stairway to my classroom, I heard, "Good morning Mari Anne!" A very tall, pleasant-faced, Korean gentleman, dressed in a nice business suit, addressed me. He didn't have the customary Korean accent. Usually even older Koreans who have been born in America have a slight accent. He had none! He was taller than I was. He definitely was not a local Korean.

Is he an American? I silently questioned. I had never seen this individual around our school before that moment. *Is he an angel? Is he my angel?* My mind questioned. *What does one say to an angel?*

"Good morning, sir!" I said, nodded, and gave a slight American version of the polite Korean bow. As I continued downstairs to the first-floor classroom and turned on the heat, I contemplated this unusual encounter.

After class, I ran upstairs to every classroom and asked each teacher if they had seen a very tall Korean gentleman in their classroom or the hallway? No one had seen him. I asked the secretaries. No one would have been overlooked by their observant watchfulness, but they hadn't seen the tall Korean man either! I scurried to the pastors' offices, and they'd had no such visitor! At first everyone was amused by my story, but they soon sobered and became inspired.

Did I see an angel that day? I believe I did! I'm sure God sent him to reassure us of His protecting care of our school. The thought went through my mind that angels parade the hallways of our Christian schools to keep them safe. Some of my days in Korea were extremely challenging, but exciting. After meeting the Korean angel on the stairway, I felt reassured that our heavenly Father was keeping careful watch over our school.

Would I go again? Oh yes, I would! I found it exciting and fun working in cooperation with an angel!

As told by Mari Anne J. Moore.

CHAPTER 30

Dad and the Hitchhiker

During a bone-chilling, late December afternoon, nineteen-year-old Bob shivered as he closed the hood of his 1937 Willys. That morning he had checked out of Walla Walla College, in College Place, Washington, with only enough money for gas to reach his parents' home in Lodi, California.

As he neared Biggs Junction, Oregon, a sudden clunking sound grabbed his attention. He quickly pulled off the road to investigate. He found that the generator had broken loose and fallen off. He realized he now needed a new generator. Even if there had been a repair shop in Biggs Junction, he had no money for a new generator. Had there been a motel to spend the night, he had no money for a room.

Darkness fell fast. The only way he could keep traveling would be to follow the taillights of other cars. He would use his headlights only when cars approached from the opposite direction. Bob pulled onto the highway behind the first car that came along and tried to keep up. But soon his car fell far behind, forcing him to stop beside the road when he could no longer see.

As Bob waited for another vehicle to come by, snow began to fall gently. Finally a semi-truck came along, and Bob pulled onto the road, following the truck in the darkness. As the distance widened between them, the Willys slid off an icy curve and went over a small embankment. His vehicle stuck fast in the snow, Bob stood in the dark beside the road, waiting for someone to drive by.

After what seemed like hours, he saw approaching headlights. Quickly, he turned on his dimming car lights as the other car approached. The traveler passed as if he had not seen the dim taillights in the ditch. After another car passed, Bob realized that his taillights were too far over the bank to be seen by other vehicle occupants. Bob prayed earnestly for help.

Another car approached. Again Bob turned on his lights. His disappointment grew as he watched the car drive by, leaving him alone in the cold night. But as he watched that car drive farther down the road, he saw the brake lights come on. To his great relief, the car turned around and returned. A couple with a young boy climbed out of the car.

The mother explained, "Our son looked back as we passed your car and saw your lights. He persuaded me to turn around and see if you needed help." She awakened her sleeping husband, who got out of the car to investigate Bob's situation. It became clear that pulling the Willys out of the ditch would be too difficult for their small car.

As they stood on the road pondering what to do next, they saw the flashing yellow light of a snowplow far in the distance.

The snowplow would be just what they needed to pull Bob's car out of the ditch. This family drove Bob to the snowplow. The snowplow driver offered to pull the Willys from the ditch. Once again Bob was on the road. This time he followed the snowplow. Unfortunately, the snowplow driver didn't notice that the little Willys dropped farther and farther behind. All too soon, Bob was again parked beside the road.

This time a car soon came by, and Bob followed, straining to see the road. Never in his young life had a night seemed so long and cold. Never before had Bob wished more and more to be at home in his warm bed.

By the time he reached Bend, Oregon, dawn tinted the horizon. He noticed a hitchhiker standing beside the road in the cold early morning. With a grateful heart for the kindness shown to him during that long night, he stopped to share kindness with someone else in need. The man climbed into the car, and together they traveled toward California.

As they descended the mountainous pass into the central valley of California, the sun came through the windshield, warming and relaxing the chilled travelers. After being awake all night, Bob grew sleepy. He started to doze. Suddenly he snapped back to alertness as the hitchhiker grabbed the wheel, steering it precariously between a freight truck and a telephone pole. Realizing he had missed death by inches and seconds kept Bob wide awake for the remaining miles to Sacramento.

Near Sacramento, the hitchhiker turned to Bob and said, "I'll get out here. You'll be all right now the rest of the way, I'm sure." Bob stopped and let the stranger out. As Bob drove away, a strange and thrilling thought came to his mind. Was the hitchhiker his guardian angel? Had God sent that hitchhiker to keep him awake? Or was he just a man God used to save his life from a fatal accident? Something about the way the hitchhiker had spoken to Bob while they traveled lingered in Bob's memory as the words of a heavenly messenger.

Upon arriving home that evening, Bob told his family what had happened to him on his way. As they listened, their hearts overflowed, and they thanked God for keeping Bob safe. For many years, Bob has faithfully served the God who cares about each of us individually. Occasionally our heavenly Father reveals His miraculous care through angels in the form of common men, to encourage in us a greater faith and joy.

By Donna Kohfeld, as told by her father, Bob Battee.

CHAPTER 31

We Discovered God's Power

Nineteen excited teenagers and their counselors—members of the Kelowna, British Columbia, Silver-Tip Pathfinder Club—left town on August 4, 1999, in an eleven-passenger van and a motor home. Our destination? The International Pathfinder Camporee in Oshkosh, Wisconsin, U.S.A.

Everyone enjoyed the trip. Some evenings we reached our prearranged campsites much later than planned. But we were still on schedule by Friday, and we anticipated arriving at North Dakota Adventist Academy before sundown. Then the unexpected happened! Our motor home quietly lost power and coasted to the side of the road. We had no idea what was wrong! But as events unfolded, we were to witness God working miracle after miracle.

Two days before we had left home, we were impressed to increase our British Columbia Automobile Association roadside coverage for our motor home. (BCAA is an automobile association similar to AAA in the United States.) The increase would provide towing of an RV and increased the covered towing distance from twenty miles to one hundred miles.

We had just passed a small town in North Dakota when the motor home developed its problem, and by BCAA rules we should have been towed back to the nearest garage. While we waited for the tow truck to arrive, we prayed, "Please God, get us to our destination somehow!"

The tow truck driver suggested we call and negotiate with BCAA. We did, and our prayers were answered. BCAA agreed that we could be towed to Bismarck, which was precisely one hundred miles away. Our family stayed there and slept in the motor home at the Chevrolet dealership. The rest of the group traveled on to the academy and arrived there at midnight.

The next morning we were disappointed to discover that the dealership would not have time to diagnose the motor home's problem until Monday. We needed to be in Oshkosh—eight hundred miles away—by Tuesday!

We called car rental companies and found that none had an eight-passenger vehicle available. Besides, a rental would cost us more than $1,600, and our club had no extra money for that kind of expense. We tried to sell the motor home, but the offers were ridiculously low. The Chevrolet dealer had no suitable used vehicle. We asked the academy if we could borrow a school van for one week, but the answer was negative.

Finally the dealer loaned us a car and gave us a list of about six used car lots. After visiting three of them, we got discouraged. Providentially, we ended up at a Ford dealer that wasn't even on our list. We walked through the lot of used vehicles, and there on the back row we discovered an Astro marked $1,320. The keys were in it, and we started it. As we wondered why the price was so low, a salesman approached. He allowed us to test drive the van, and we decided to purchase it.

We didn't have that amount of cash, so we asked the dealer, "May we charge it to our Master Card?"

He said, "No!"

We explained our situation and tried to impress them with how important this vehicle was to us. When we mentioned a Canadian check, the dealer began to get creative in order to avoid Canadian funds. Shortly, it was decided the charge could be put through the parts department on our Master Card. Technically, we bought one large, self-propelled "part." It was exactly what we needed. Again we saw God's hand at work in our behalf.

Our next problem was to obtain registration and insurance. The dealer gave us the customary North Dakota drive-out registration, valid for one month. Insurance coverage was not as easy to acquire. We learned that at noon virtually all the businesses in Bismarck would be closed until Monday morning. The local insurance company could not insure out-of-country visitors. We called our insurance company in British Columbia. Fortunately it agreed to cover us with insurance until we got home. Again, we saw God at work for us. We realized how much He cared for us and saw His ultimate power to solve our problems. Sunday morning, we left on schedule, but our adventures continued.

Sunday night before we set up our tents at Maplewood Academy, fifty miles west of Minneapolis, one of our staff felt impressed to ask the boys' dean, "Are there any empty dorm rooms available?"

"Yes, as a matter of fact, we do have empty rooms available." Everyone in our group obtained a room in the dorm.

As we prepared supper, a windstorm grew stronger and stronger. During the night a tremendous prairie thunderstorm with torrents of rain passed over us. How grateful we were to be safe inside of the dorm instead of out in tents!

Due to the heavy rain, we didn't stop to eat in Minneapolis the next morning. An hour later, we stopped at a restaurant. While we ate, it grew very dark outside. We believe our angels took us off the interstate highway to keep us safe from what was probably a tornado raging through the countryside. In spite of the difficulties along the way, we arrived at Oshkosh on schedule and settled into our tents. We were off to a great Camporee! The evening program portrayed how young people can choose Jesus to help them resist the devil.

Shortly after getting into bed about 11:15 P.M., we heard sirens. Camporee leaders hurried through camp on golf carts shouting, "Run to the red barn! A tornado is coming right for us!" We scrambled out of bed and ran. While running toward the barn we noticed the wind had stopped. It was scary!

Later, the Camporee director recounted how the air traffic control operators at Oshkosh watched the radar in amazement as the storm split into two parts, passing on either side of the 22,000 campers, and later joined back together to race on its way. Large hail, approximately one inch in diameter, extensively damaged crops and property north of the camp. God protected His young campers and showed them His power! I can picture angels standing on the south side of the camp with their shields held high saying, "No farther, Satan!

You can't destroy these kids. You'll have to go around them with your storm!"

Our Camporee concluded Saturday evening with an incredible display of fireworks! Sunday morning at 6:00 A.M. our van headed back to Bismarck to pick up the motor home. At about 8:00 P.M. we drove through some very heavy, black clouds and pouring rain. As we drove west, the sun broke through the clouds. Looking back, we saw some of the most awesome cloud formations. Later at a rest area, a trucker told us that we had just passed through the edge of a tornado! A feeling of awe swept over us. We had truly discovered God's power during our entire trip to Oshkosh, Wisconsin, and the Pathfinder Camporee!

As told by Elizabeth Odiyar.

CHAPTER 32

A Promise Fulfilled

"Dear God," Irene prayed. "Am I going to die? Who will raise my little girls?"

Just that morning, the doctor had told her parents, "I'm sorry to have to tell you this, but she won't last more than a few weeks. Could you reach her husband? I realize he's on a submarine in the South Pacific somewhere, and it may prove difficult to reach him."

Irene's heart had never been strong. She was a sickly child, and doctors had predicted she'd never live to be a teenager. But she fought her way through respiratory illnesses and nervous disorders. As always, her weak heart overshadowed her life.

But she did survive and married when she was seventeen. In the next few years Irene even gave birth to two daughters. However, she continued to be weak, sickly, and often bedridden— "puny" was one word people used to describe her.

Now, at age twenty-four, Irene lay in a hospital bed wavering between life and death. Private duty nurses watched over her night and day.

Doctors had delivered her third daughter two days earlier. But twelve hours after birth, the baby died; her heart wasn't strong enough to survive.

"Irene's heart isn't strong enough either," the medical staff told her family.

About ten days after the death of her baby, Irene lay awake in the middle of the night, wondering what the future held for her, begging God for her own life. Her parents had gone home. Even her nurse had just stepped out of the room for a bite to eat. Irene felt so alone.

"Please, God," she cried again. "Don't let me die!"

Suddenly, the darkness began to fade. The room grew brighter and brighter until the whole room was filled with light! Irene blinked her eyes, trying to see who had turned on the light. But the overhead light wasn't on. What was happening?

As she strained her eyes to see the source of the light, she could just make out the form of a very tall man, with white, shimmering wings, standing beside her bed! Irene stared open-mouthed.

The angel reached over and took her hand. Then in the kindest voice she had ever heard, he said, "Everything's going to be all right, Irene."

She clung to his hand for a moment. Then he gently removed it and stepped back. The light faded. The angel was gone. Darkness once again filled the room.

The nurse returned to find her patient excited and trying to sit up. She babbled about getting better, getting well, and living!

The nurse reported that Irene's medications needed to be adjusted; she was getting delusional. The next week Irene was moved to a sanitarium, still with private duty nurses. But in spite of the doctor's predictions, she slowly grew stronger. Two weeks later, Irene went home!

People laughed when she told them of the angel's visit.

"You were dreaming!" one said.

"Probably a reaction to the medication," said another.

But Irene held fast to the angel's promise for recovery.

Irene recently turned eighty-six years old. She has to depend on a walker these days for stability when she walks. Her hands are twisted with arthritis. But she claims that she is healthier than she has ever been. She happily knits sweaters and caps for the homeless and afghans for bazaars. She plays a mean game of Scrabble and reads a lot. She remembers everyone's birthday, attends church regularly, and loves to eat in restaurants. In addition to all that, she checks the spelling and grammar in this author's manuscripts.

You see, Irene Leach is my mother, and I praise God that the angel's promise came true!

As written by Sandy Zaugg.

CHAPTER 33

A Head of Lettuce

Verna gasped as the checker at the supermarket said, "That will be $3.76, please." The change from her five-dollar bill looked forlornly meager as she dropped it into her purse. Once outside the market she remarked to her sister, Raylene, "There must be a mistake. Surely those few items of groceries couldn't have cost that much!"

"Well, let's check it out," Raylene suggested. "Except for the lettuce, the prices are on each item."

As Verna compared the receipt with the contents in the shopping bag she exclaimed, "Look, Raylene, this shows the lettuce cost fifty-four cents. I can't believe it—fifty-four cents for one little head of lettuce! At that rate how can Dad manage to feed our family of six and keep up with all our other expenses, too?"

"Maybe that's why he's planting such a big garden this spring. Let's go home and suggest he plant several more rows of lettuce." Raylene quickened her step in harmony with her words.

During the summer, it fell to the lot of Verna and Raylene to help hoe and weed that extra-large garden. There were times they wished they could be relieved of the chore, but the memory of the fifty-four-cent head of lettuce would return and revive their lagging interest.

Their responsibility included more than hoeing and weeding. When the pods plumped up on the pea vines, they had to pick them and help shell the roly-poly peas. It was job enough to shell out a kettleful for a family of six, but it didn't stop there.

"Dad sure had the freezer in mind when he planted all those rows of peas, didn't he?" Raylene remarked as she doggedly continued, breaking open pod after pod.

Verna heaved a big sigh, but quickly reminded Raylene, "They'll help cut down on the grocery bill this winter, though, when Dad is struggling to pay tuition for four of us."

A concerned wrinkle creased Raylene's forehead as she said, "I wonder whether lettuce will still be fifty-four cents a head by that time."

"Probably even higher. It's too bad Mom can't find a way to store some of the lettuce we've raised this summer." Verna glanced out toward the garden. "But anyway, with a good crop of corn, our freezer is really going to bulge. Won't it be nice to be eating home-grown corn through the winter months!" A smile of happy anticipation played around the corners of her mouth.

The summer wore on, and it came time for Dad to attend college for a short refresher course before September, when he would resume teaching at the academy.

"Do you think you girls and Mother can handle the garden in my absence?" he asked.

"We'll do our best, Dad," Verna answered. As the memory of a certain head of lettuce flashed through her mind, she added, "We can't let a single thing go to waste out there—not with food prices what they are."

All went well for the next few weeks. There were lots of canning and freezing of garden produce. Then one morning a letter came from Dad stating he would be through with his studies earlier than expected and would like for the family to join him for a vacation in the mountains. What a treat this promised to be!

"What camping supplies will we need?"

"Can we begin packing now?"

"I need a new sleeping bag, Mother."

Amidst all of this happy planning, Verna suddenly stopped short. She noticed Mother looking out the window with a troubled expression on her face. Crossing the room to stand beside her, she saw the tall green stalks on the far side of the garden.

"Oh, Mom!" she exclaimed. "What about the corn? Will it be ready for the freezer before we leave?"

"That's just what I was wondering," Mother answered. "Let's go out and look it over."

They walked down several rows, feeling the most likely ears. Verna asked anxiously, "What do you think, Mom?"

The answer was not the one she was hoping for. "Well, it looks discouraging. It's my guess it will take at least ten days before any is ready, and it's less than a week before we leave. What is equally discouraging is that it will be overripe by the time we return."

Verna lay awake a long time that night thinking about their beautiful patch of sweet corn and how much they needed to save it. That fifty-four-cent head of lettuce continued to drive home its lesson on economy. At last she told herself, *Why am I lying here worrying about the corn? Jesus knows our problem, and He is the very One who can do something about it.* She remembered hearing that prayer is the key in the hand of faith to unlock heaven's storehouse. *Power from heaven's storehouse is just what that corn needs to give it the extra boost it has to have to make it ready to harvest before we leave on vacation,* she thought. With that, she offered up a prayer, and then sank into peaceful slumber.

The next few days passed by one by one—cool days that did little to hasten the filling out of those precious kernels of corn. Still Mother, Verna, Raylene, and the two younger boys continued to pray for the unlocking of heaven's storehouse.

Wednesday morning dawned with rosy streaks in the eastern sky. When Verna awakened, her first thought was, *Will today bring the answer to our prayers? Tomorrow will be too late, for we must leave early to join Dad.*

What a busy day it was! Besides packing, they had to drive thirty miles to town to get Aunt Julie, who was going camping with them, and to do some last-minute shopping. It was late in the afternoon before they returned home.

Mother instructed the girls, "You two give Aunt Julie a hand with her luggage while I get some food on the table. I know you're all half starved."

Verna, whose thoughts and prayers had been with the corn patch throughout the day, ventured, "Maybe if we check the corn, we can have a few roasting ears."

Without a word Mother rushed out to the garden. Her face was radiant when she returned. She was carrying more than the few roasting ears.

"Children," she said with awe in her voice, "Something wonderful has happened. There are many, many ears of corn ready for picking. Our prayers have been answered!"

The evening meal was one of true thanksgiving, and immediately following it the whole family began processing corn. Package after package was plopped into the freezer. No one noticed how late it was getting as they worked on and on. Every so often, someone would burst forth singing the children's song, "Praise Him, praise Him, all ye little children, God is good, God is good." A special Bible verse came to mind, "Casting all your care upon him; for he careth for you" (I Peter 5:7, KJV). It was the most thrilling work bee any of them could remember.

The next morning as the family and Aunt Julie loaded the camping gear into the car, they paused to look at the garden.

"You know, Mom," Verna observed, "that garden has supplied us with two blessings. An abundance of food and a wonderful experience in answered prayer. Right?"

"Exactly right!" Mother responded heartily.

Written by Mabel Latsha.
First published in Guide, *Volume 22, Number 21.*
Used by permission.

CHAPTER 34

Guilty Fingers

Louise heard the "beep-beep" of the car horn. Yes, she knew they should be leaving for church immediately, but where was her watch?

I left it lying right here in the usual place. Why can't I find it?

"Beep-beep," sounded a second time. *Oh, well, I'll get along without it this morning.* She quickly joined her family in the car.

"I couldn't find my watch, Mother. Did you see it anywhere?"

"Why, no, dear," her mother replied, "but you know I've always warned you not to leave it lying so carelessly on the dish cupboard. That's no place for a watch. It could get knocked about so easily."

Louise agreed. "I know, but it's so handy to slip it off my arm and into the cupboard when I'm ready to wash dishes. I'm sure it's still there, probably hidden behind some of the cups and saucers."

It was a day or two later before Louise got around to making a real search for the watch. She moved everything in the cupboard and even looked inside each cup and deep dish. But no watch. She emptied out the two purses she had been using. She searched through dresser drawers and any place she thought it at all possible she might have put the watch.

"Oh, Mother," she said dolefully. "I hate to think I'd never find that watch again. Remember how long I saved to get it? Why, only last week I was looking at it and thinking of how it has never given me one bit of trouble in the three years I've had it."

"Yes, I know you are really fond of it. I'll help you look for it. It's bound to be in the house somewhere, unless . . ."

As her mother paused, Louise seemed to read her mind. "Are you beginning to consider the same ugly possibility I am—that Edith might have picked it up when she was here last Friday?"

Mother hesitated. "Well, for the time being let's leave it as only a possibility. She seemed like such a good girl. But you know, we've been told of things she has picked up in other homes, and a reputation of that kind surely follows you."

"I know," Louise responded, "but I've been trying hard to forget those reports and just enjoy her friendship." She cast a wistful glance toward the dish cupboard.

Another thorough search. Again no watch.

"Do we have to conclude that Edith is guilty of stealing it?" Louise asked with reluctance in her voice.

"Well, the only other guest in our home last week was Arlene, and I feel positive she would never do such a thing. With poor Edith's record of guilty fingers, there is ground for suspicion. But let's go slowly. Let's ask the Lord to direct us in finding that watch if it is at all possible."

Two more days passed by with Louise becoming more convinced of Edith's guilt. She wondered whether she should come right out and ask her about the watch in a nice way or first tell the pastor about the matter and ask for his advice. Because she wanted to handle the matter in a Christian way, she did some reading on how to relate to others. A quotation from *Steps to Christ* especially impressed her.

Keeping her finger on page 121, she joined her mother in the kitchen where she was kneading bread dough into loaves. "Mother," Louise announced, "I've found a quotation I want to read to you. It seems to be written just for me at this time: 'We should love and respect one another, notwithstanding the faults and imperfections that we cannot help seeing. Humility and self-distrust should be cultivated, and a patient tenderness with the faults of others.' "

Louise fell silent for a second, and then said, "It hurts me to think that Edith would deliberately take my watch, but I'm going to do my best with the Lord's help to keep from feeling any bitterness toward her."

As Mother brushed the tops of the loaves of bread with oil, she answered, "You're right about that, Louise. However, you surely haven't forgotten that the evidence we have against her is purely circumstantial. We may yet find she is completely innocent."

Louise laid down her book and tossed the snowy white cloth over the rising loaves of bread. "That's true, yet I can't think of another place in this house to look for that watch, and I've honestly tried to recall the last time I wore it and where I put it."

With a sigh she picked up the book and returned it to the bookcase. As she sat down on the piano bench close by, a simple prayer arose from the depths of her heart: "Oh Lord, You know exactly where my watch is. If Edith is innocent of taking it, please help me find it and clear away our doubts."

A new thought began to take shape in Louise's mind. A slight frown appeared on her brow, and then gave way to a smile.

"Mother!" she called excitedly as she dashed into the kitchen. "What day was it I picked huckleberries with Arlene's family?"

There was a tinge of surprise in Mother's voice as she replied, "It was last Thursday. Why do you ask?"

Louise's only answer was, "Wait!" as she rushed straight to the clothes closet in her room. A moment later she reappeared in the kitchen, triumphantly carrying the little watch! The gladness and relief Louise felt radiated right out through her words as she exclaimed, "It's found, Mother, it's found! Oh, I'm so happy! Yet I feel guilty for having felt sure Edith had taken it."

Her mother smiled. "Don't feel too bad about it, dear. You had reasons for supposing that could be the case because Edith has allowed a bad habit to control her from time to time. The main thing now is that we can be grateful she's been proved innocent. But, tell me, what did picking huckleberries have to do with finding the watch?"

"Well, it could only be that the Lord awakened my thoughts, for I had completely forgotten that I took my old worn-out straw purse to the woods on Thursday. I never use it anymore. But I carried it that day for Band-Aids and such. I can remember clearly now that I also put my watch in there so that we could know when it was time to start home. I didn't want to wear it among the bushes. When we found there weren't many berries, we came home early without having to check my watch, and I never thought of it again."

As Mother set the oven temperature for the bread, she spoke reverently: "Well, this all goes to prove how much the Lord concerns Himself with our daily problems, and how close He is to us at all times."

"But, Mother," Louise said with earnestness, "it seems strange He waited so long before causing me to remember the straw purse." Then she brightened. "But if He had answered my prayer at the beginning, I never would have run across the beautiful statement in *Steps to Christ* on humility, and self-distrust, and patient tenderness."

Written by Mabel Latsha.
Published in Guide, *Volume 22, Number 13.*
Used by permission.

CHAPTER 35

Angels Are Real!

Early in 1920, our family lived in Innisfree, Alberta, Canada, east of Edmonton. At ages two and four, respectively, my sister and I became seriously ill. The nearest doctor was fifty miles away, and we had no means of transportation to get there. One day Mr. Smith, a graduate nurse from Battle Creek, Michigan, visited our home. He'd recently bought a farm in our community. When Mr. Smith discovered that my sister Anne and I were almost breathing our last, he suggested to our parents, "Call the elder of the Seventh-day Adventist Church. Ask him to anoint and pray for your sick girls."

In desperation, Father called the elder, who anointed us and prayed. The result? At once we were completely healed! Our gratitude to God for His healing has been unfailing ever since that time. For the rest of my life this experience produced a strong faith in God's leading and intervention.

After that miraculous childhood recovery, I remained healthy until May 1949, when I went to see two doctors at the Edmonton

University Hospital of Alberta. My mother accompanied me. After completing their examination of my problem, they told me, "It's too late! The kidney stone infection has progressed much too far! There is no hope or help!"

"But I insist you do surgery immediately and remove the kidney stone!" Mother demanded. Her insistence paid off. I was in surgery four and a half hours, but after a slow recovery, I'm still here more than fifty years later, thanks to God!

After surgery, I was placed in a large ward with eighteen other patients. For the first week, I subsisted only on intravenous feedings. By the time Sabbath arrived, I missed the "Sabbath" atmosphere of home. One patient continuously played cheap music on her large radio. I was sick and weary of listening to that music all week. So I covered my head with the sheet and wept.

Suddenly, I no longer heard the cheap music blaring. Instead I heard beautiful singing—the entire song, "Abide With Me." After that beautiful hymn ended, I uncovered my head and heard the radio music again.

When I told some friends about this incident, one said, "Helen, that was the angels singing for you, don't you think?" To this day I remember that beautiful singing. It proved a great blessing to me.

By March 1950, I'd recovered sufficiently and it was time for me to find a job. I packed my belongings and traveled by train three thousand miles across Canada to Toronto, Ontario. Once I arrived in Toronto, I readily found a job at the T. Eaton Company. I enjoyed working on the twelfth floor ironing men's ties and scarves. The Eaton Company was a great place to work, I found.

Previous to my serious illness I had spent a successful year during 1945 to 1946 selling Christian books and magazines door to door in Alberta. After my surgery, I felt I wasn't physically fit for that type of work. All went well with my work at Eaton. But in my mind I felt God calling me to sell Christian books and magazines again. I resisted the thought each time I felt the Lord's urgent call.

One day, I was late leaving work at quitting time. Mabel, my supervisor, and I were the last to leave. The elevator man waited for us as we hurriedly approached. After we got in, something went wrong. The elevator plunged downward totally out of control! Just before we hit bottom, the operator was able to bring it to a stop. This frightening incident caused me to begin thinking seriously. I realized that God had spared my life, and I felt that I owed my life to Him. I felt an inner voice urging me to resume selling Christian books and magazines door to door as I had done previously.

Finally, I gave Eaton notice that I would be quitting my job. The company raised my wages because they did not want me to leave. A second time, I gave them my notice; again they raised my wages. This enticed me to stay and continue working. Finally, I handed in my resignation for the third time. The foreman said, "She has seriously made up her mind to leave, so we'll let her go!"

For almost a year, I sold Christian books and magazines in Toronto along with two other young ladies. My sister, Janet, cooked for the three of us while we sold books house to house. Near the end of the summer of 1952, the field secretary who supervised our selling asked me to go to northern Ontario with another girl to sell books there. I consented and got ready to go in three days. I took the train to Timmins, a gold mining town about 160 miles from James Bay on the Arctic Ocean. My partner and I sold books in that area until November, when it turned cold and the snow came up to our knees. We returned to Toronto and continued our sales work. While I sold books, I remained strong and healthy. I carried thirty pounds of books and at times walked fifteen miles a day going from house to house.

Near Simcoe, Ontario, I sold books to tobacco farmers. During the time I worked there, I also "house sat" for a family who took a trip to British Columbia to visit relatives. I did a few chores, ate from their garden, and sold books to their neighbors. The first day after the family left, I sold books all day and got home late that afternoon. After I arrived home, I put down my purse and briefcase and hurried to the basement to get the margarine. This family did not have a refrigerator, and Mrs. K. had shown me where they kept the margarine in the basement. The entrance to the basement was outdoors. I had picked up the margarine and started up the stairs, when I almost ran into a young fellow about seventeen years old, holding a big shotgun in his hands. He stopped and stared at me. I asked him, "What do you want? Who are you looking for?"

"I'm looking for the black crow," he answered, referring to my black hair. He was near the top of the steps, and I near the bottom. Suddenly, he looked both ways, and whatever he saw made him run, gun in hand, into the bushes adjacent to the house. Apparently, he saw something I didn't. I'm sure it must have been my guardian angel! Even though the man didn't return, I felt very uneasy sleeping alone in that large house. Each time I awoke that night, I prayed, "Please, Lord, send a legion of angels to protect me." Finally I slept the rest of the night.

The next day I told Mr. K's mother about my young visitor and his gun. She lived only a quarter mile away and suggested, "Come sleep at my house nights. In the morning you can go back to their house to feed the dog and chickens, have your breakfast, bathe, and get ready to sell your books." I followed her suggestion and was grateful for her hospitality. For one month I stayed there without a phone. The Lord protected me, and I was not bothered by anyone for the rest of the time I stayed at that home.

One day while going door to door, I found most people weren't at home. They all seemed to be out in their fields picking tobacco leaves. When I started toward home late in the day, I began finding folks at home. I obtained book orders at nearly every home, but when I stopped to check the time, I found it was much too late to be out. I hurried back home. I quickly fed the dog, gathered the eggs, and fed the chickens. I had promised to deliver a book that evening to a customer who lived two miles away. I grabbed the book and hurried down the driveway to make that delivery. As soon as I reached the road, I noticed that the dog left his meal and trotted along with me, but on the opposite side of the road.

I threw a few pebbles at him, shouting, "Go home! Go home!" But he wouldn't leave me. When I arrived at my destination, the dog lay down by the gate and waited while I made the delivery. As soon as I started for home, the dog got up and walked beside me all the way home. The first mile was a paved road, but the next mile was gravel lined with tall trees making an archway overhead. The sun had just set. It was pitch black, and I didn't have a flashlight. Now I felt glad to have the dog right beside me—his head up, sniffing the air. I smelled tobacco smoke and heard twigs snapping as though someone were walking nearby. Now I understood why the dog was led to accompany me. As I turned into Mr. K's mother's house for the night, the dog left me to keep walking homeward.

During the ten years I sold Christian books, I enjoyed every challenge it brought to me. I will always thank the Lord for His protection over me during those years. He has always been an ever-present Friend. Some day, in that better land, I am looking forward to meeting my guardian angel and listening to him tell me of the many times he saved me from dangerous situations during those years I sold books. I want to thank him personally for his guidance and protection throughout my entire life. I know angels are real!

As told by Helen Hyrchuk-Bishop.

CHAPTER 36

Call Upon Me

A brisk wind blew against us as we stood gazing intently into the sky, completely unmindful of its chill. At that moment it was as though we'd been transported back to the shores of the Red Sea, standing beside Moses, beholding the miracle of the waters rolled back by the hand of God that His people might pass through in safety. Except that in this case it was not water that had been rolled back; it was clouds. Instead of dry ground for a passageway, it was clear, blue sky! And there wasn't a great company of people involved—only one small family of five in a Piper Pacer airplane.

Can we expect God to perform miracles for a group so few in number in this modern age? I can only relate the circumstances as they happened, allowing you to draw your own conclusions.

My husband and I live in the Redwood area of northern California, sixty miles south of Eureka. Our son, Donald, a faculty member at Upper Columbia Academy near Spokane, Washington, and his family had flown down to visit us. Carefully he checked flying conditions with the weather bureau. The report was, "Morning fog with early clearing over the weekend." This weather pattern had persisted for several days, so it was with confidence that we settled down for a happy time together. However, other conditions were developing that were beyond our control.

We awakened Saturday morning to find ourselves engulfed in rain clouds. By noon, the fine misty rain had turned into intermittent snow flurries. This surprise storm had sneaked in unannounced. All afternoon we fervently hoped it would depart as suddenly as it had arrived.

That evening friends came to visit and brought a transistor radio with them, which gave us frequent weather reports. For the next three hours we turned to it often. The reports were not good. The entire northwest section of the United States was in the clutches of heavy rain, snow, ice, and blizzards. After our friends with the transistor radio went home, we knew that the Piper Pacer waiting at the Rhonerville airport, near Fortuna, would not be flying the next morning.

"How could the report for an 'all clear weekend' get so fouled up?" Don asked dejectedly. "I need to be back at the academy to work Monday morning!"

That's when we realized that we were in much the same position as the Israelites at the Red Sea. There they were—helpless to do anything for themselves, surrounded by sea, mountains, and the approaching Egyptian army. We, too, were entirely helpless to do anything about the disturbed elements around us. But this we knew: The One who made a path through the Red Sea for the Israelites was just as able to make a path through the clouds for Don and his family today.

Remembering the Scripture, "God is our refuge and strength, a very present help in trouble" (Psalm 46:1, KJV), we knelt and placed the situation in the hands of our heavenly Father, asking that His will be done. We all retired with calmness and peace in our hearts.

The night was short because the alarm rang at 3:30 A.M. Don arose and telephoned the Eureka Weather Bureau for a report on the latest flying conditions. All routes were completely closed—except the most unlikely one. The pathway up the Oregon coast—prone to prevailing fog—was clear. But another storm front was moving in toward Portland.

The man at the Weather Bureau told Don, "If you get started immediately, you probably could get beyond Portland before the next storm front arrives."

We lost no time getting packed and on the road to the Rhonerville airport. Fog enveloped us all the way through the wooded area along Highway 101. But as we neared the Rhonerville turnoff, our hearts thrilled with gratefulness; there was no fog, and all was clear. This was the reassurance we needed to realize that the Lord was making a way through the clouds for Don and his family. The Old Testament accounts of God's faithfulness, guidance, and watch care over His people became more precious to us than ever.

As quickly as possible we swept the ice from the wings of the plane, loaded the baggage, warmed up the motor, and belted in Don's little family for the takeoff. Soon their plane roared down the runway and lifted. They gained altitude, circled, flew high over our heads, and turned toward the coast. Silently we stood watching the plane grow smaller and smaller until it became but a speck in the sky and soon blended into the atmosphere. They were gone from our sight, yet we knew that God's eye was still upon them.

Thus it was that we stood in the icy wind without feeling its chilling effect. To us this was our Red Sea experience, and it was awesome! Don and his family reached their destination in record time. They flew up the coast to Portland, and then up the Columbia Gorge toward Spokane. Heavy fog both to the north and south of them eventually closed in, but not until they were safely beyond it. Over the plane's radio came reports that all planes were grounded in those areas that lay immediately behind them. They marveled at the wonderful way God carried them through ahead of the storm! In awe they wondered as did the psalmist, "What is man, that thou art mindful of him? and the son of man, that thou visitest him?" (Psalm 8:4, KJV). From the depths of their hearts they thanked the Lord for His great goodness to them that day!

It is comforting to feel God is near in our physical perplexities. It is still more comforting, and of far greater importance, to call upon Him for our spiritual needs. You and I are travelers, wanting to reach our heavenly home. It often seems that we will be grounded by the storms of life closing in about us. If we have made sure that our flight plans are filed with our heavenly Father, we need not fear. No matter how turbulent our surroundings or how dense the clouds of sin, a way of escape has been made, and He will carry us through to safety just as He saw Don and his family through that day in their Piper Pacer plane!

As written by Mabel Latsha.

CHAPTER 37

The Lord's Impression

After my husband completed college, his first pastoral assignment included three churches in northern Alberta, Canada. We moved to a small town that had no church members living in it. Our nearest church was fifty miles from our home. The other two churches were located even farther away.

We began our pastoral work by visiting the people in our community and inviting them to attend the evangelistic meetings we planned to hold in our town.

One cold, wintry day we headed out into the country on roads deep with snow. We planned to visit the people in that area and invite them to our meetings as well. Suddenly we came upon a crossroad. We stopped our car and asked the Lord, "Please guide us in the choice of which road we are to take. Lord, You know which roads are open for travel. We have quite a distance to go. You know, too, if we get stuck, there would be no one close by to help us." At that time, no telephones were available in that part of the country.

After our prayer, the Lord impressed us to take the road to the right. We followed the road and found it passable all the way to a friend's home. After a nice visit, we were thankful to have returned home safely from the country over the snow-filled roads.

A few days later when the roads were opened, we drove to visit another family, this time taking the road to the left at the same crossroad. We told the people that we had intended to visit them a few days earlier, but had been impressed by the Lord to visit the family on the right instead.

"It's a good thing you didn't come to visit us on that day," the husband told us, "because two of our neighbors were waiting for you with big clubs, pastor. They planned to beat you so that you would never speak again, let alone preach!"

We have thanked the Lord over and over again for sending His angel to direct us which road to take that day at the cross-road! We had no idea that two men were planning to harm us. Throughout the many years of our pastoral work, God has been so good in protecting and guiding us—just as He promised in Psalm 32:8, "I will instruct thee and teach thee in the way which thou shalt go: I will guide thee with mine eye" (KJV).

As told by Anne Samograd.

CHAPTER 38

Who Was the Stranger?

Only one more hour and we would be home! We hadn't seen this much traffic since leaving home two months earlier. Now, carefully maneuvering our thirty-foot motor home towing our car, we merged onto the 210 freeway in Pasadena, California. Cars and trucks surrounded us on the eight lanes of highway— four going each direction. Rounding a curve, we saw a large cardboard box in the road ahead of us. We couldn't stop in the fast-moving traffic without being hit from behind. With cars on all sides of us, there was no place to go.

We hit the box hoping it was empty. Parts of it flew in all directions, but the box wasn't empty. Even though we had now slowed to a crawl we could hear something dragging beneath us and grating on the concrete. Finally we were able to get to the outside lane, but there was no place to pull off and park. We traveled about a block to an off ramp before being able to get off the highway far enough to park and see what was dragging underneath our RV.

My husband, Oscar, hopped out to take a look and came right back. "I've got to change my shirt and crawl underneath to free the muffler of what looks like a large cushion that is stuck fast. Under the cushion is a plywood board attached. That's probably what made the scraping sound. I hope I don't need help to get it all loose."

Thinking that I would be the most likely one to help, if help were required, I went out the door to take a look. As I descended the steps, I saw a man on a beautiful Arabian horse riding up from the canyon on our right.

He called to me, "Are you having trouble with your motor home?"

"I don't know," I replied. "We hit a box on the freeway, and something is caught on the muffler."

The stranger rode his horse around to the other side of the motor home and dismounted. He handed me the reins. While I stroked the horse's long neck, the stranger crawled under the motor home and easily pulled the large cushion from the muffler. The cushion was charred and smoldering from the heat of the muffler. He placed it away from the motor home next to a nearby fence.

Oscar had just changed his clothes and had come out in time to thank the stranger, who told us, "Your muffler is a little loose, but I couldn't see any other damage." He mounted his horse and rode toward the underpass.

As we entered the RV, I told Oscar, "His horse was sweaty. We need to give it a drink." We turned to call to the stranger and offer his horse a drink, but there was no horse and rider in sight anywhere!

Everything happened so fast, we hadn't even thought to breathe a prayer to thank God for sparing us from an accident. Here God had sent someone to help us and supplied our need. We don't know whether the stranger was an angel—it seems so. But it could have been a kind human being too; we're not sure. But we were shown that we don't ever need to think that we can solve all of our problems by ourselves. "And it shall come to pass, that before they call, I will answer; and while they are yet speaking, I will hear" (Isaiah 65:24, KJV).

As told by Oralee Teske.

CHAPTER 39

Close Call

Young Donnie stood near the old combine watching his dad check the machine in preparation for the upcoming harvest. "When are you going to finish so we can go to the lake, Dad?"

"As soon as I'm done tightening these combine belts, son!"

"Good! Are you going to be done soon?" Impatience rang in Donnie's voice. To an eleven-year-old boy who was eager to go swimming, his dad's task seemed to be taking forever. When his dad moved to tighten the last belt, Donnie's patience reached its end, "Let's go, Dad! That belt is good enough!"

Dad stood back and took a final look at the belt. He thought it didn't look all that bad even though he felt that it needed a bit more tightening. But he relented to his son's coaxing and left fixing the combine, trudging after his jubilant, skipping boy.

During harvest on the Saskatchewan prairies, farmers make the most of fair weather. The drone of combines is heard day and night as precious grain is gathered into hoppers. On Sabbath, our fields remained quiet. But after sundown, my husband changed his clothes, climbed up into the combine and moved the giant machine toward the field. Since the evening was already late, he did not expect to be back until time for breakfast.

Before long the children went to bed and fell sound asleep. Soon, I also went upstairs to go to sleep. As I knelt beside my bed in prayer, I asked the Lord to be with my husband and protect him while he worked alone in the dark night. Somehow I felt uneasy about my husband's welfare. I couldn't sleep and tossed, thinking about my husband's safety. I kept claiming the promise in Psalm 34:7—"The angel of the LORD encampeth round about them that fear him, and delivereth them."

About midnight, I heard the door open downstairs and realized my husband was home. Relieved, I was surprised that he had arrived home much earlier than expected. Wearily he crawled into bed.

"What happened?" I asked.

"The belt on the combine broke," he replied.

"Too bad!" I said and rolled over. The next morning, as I went downstairs to prepare breakfast, I noticed my husband's old, work jacket hanging on the hook. A quick look at its chewed up condition told me that something more than a broken belt had happened in the night.

He came down the stairs and found me examining his jacket. "What happened last night?" I asked.

"I stopped the combine to adjust the lights," he explained. "I didn't turn off the motor, and the wind blew my jacket into an unguarded sprocket. Immediately, I was pulled toward the machine. I braced myself firmly and tried to unzip my jacket and let the machine have it. But reaching for my pocket knife, or any movement I made, drew me closer to the grinding sprocket. My skin already burned from the tightening clothing. Bracing myself with both hands on the combine against the constant pull, I couldn't do anything but pray. While I prayed, I noticed one belt was loose and slipping. I hoped it would soon break and I would be released. Finally, it did break, and I was free."

"Whew! What a close call you had!" I mopped my beaded brow with the back of my hand.

"Yes, it was a close call! If Donnie hadn't been so eager for me to take him to the lake while I was tightening that belt, it would have been too secure to give way and release me."

Isaiah 65:24 came to my mind: "Before they call, I will answer" (KJV). We learned that sometimes even young, impatient boys are used to fulfill this text.

CHAPTER 40

"I Must Tell Jesus"

In 1958, during the time that my husband was a pastor in Winnipeg, Manitoba, Canada, we took a trip to Simcoe, Ontario, to visit my sister and her family. We also planned to attend the Oshawa, Ontario, camp meeting. Because we weren't familiar with Oshawa, a family friend who was going to the same camp meeting agreed to be our guide. We followed his car with our vehicle.

About halfway to our destination, our friend stopped suddenly for a red light. My husband was traveling right behind, and his foot slipped off the brake pedal as he was stopping—and hit the gas pedal. We crashed into the back of our friend's car. The impact resulted in some serious injuries to me. My foot, ankle, and heel were smashed. My toes were severed, my leg fractured, and my knee badly injured. An ambulance raced me to the nearest hospital.

The medical staff wanted to amputate my leg, but my husband refused. Instead, it took six hours of surgery to put all of the pieces together and care for all of my extensive injuries. Before surgery began, I asked the doctor, "Please, may I pray for a successful surgery?" The doctor allowed me to pray.

After I awoke from the anesthesia, I tried to figure out where I was. A nurse dashed into my room, "Don't move! Don't move!" she said. "For the few hours you have left to live, I want to make you as comfortable as I can."

While I lay there trying to figure out what was going on, I was impressed that the angel of the Lord was right beside me. The words of the hymn "I Must Tell Jesus" came to my mind and played itself over and over again like a record player.

I spent three months in the Hamilton, Ontario, hospital and two years on crutches at our Winnipeg home. When the doctor, a specialist, released me from the hospital, he said, "You had one chance in a hundred to survive, and you took that chance!" He paused and said, "I'm sure your God helped you!"

Throughout my long recovery, I knew that my guardian angel was always at my side. This was a wonderful comfort to me. Today, I still walk with a limp, but I praise the Lord that He allowed me to live! I will be forever grateful for His unfailing help and healing during and after that serious accident.

As told by Anne Samograd.

CHAPTER 41

Who Steered Our Vehicle?

For weeks we had looked forward to our trip to British Columbia, Canada. Delighted it was finally July, we set off on our way north. First stop: Walla Walla, Washington, to visit family members. After a refreshing visit, it was hard to break away, but we were looking forward to seeing the beautiful northern mountains, and we also anticipated the spiritual feast in store for us at the Hope, British Columbia, camp meeting.

About two hours after our "goodbyes," we were driving through territory that seemed almost familiar because we had made our home near Moses Lake, Washington, fifty years before. We noticed that the highway between Moses Lake and Ephrata remained two lanes, although a few of the bumps had been removed. We had been following a pickup truck for miles, when suddenly it stopped abruptly in the road and turned on its left turn signal. Coming toward us in the opposite lane was a large, eighteen-wheeler truck. Although we had already slowed down considerably, we would not be able to stop our thirty-foot motor home with vehicle in tow in time. We had three choices—none of them good. We could head for the eighteen-wheeler; we could rear-end the pickup truck, or we could go in the ditch on the right and hope we didn't turn over. All I had time to say was, "Lord, help us!"

Oscar, my husband and driver, made the third choice. Somehow our guardian angel that excels in strength held our motor home upright as we passed the pickup truck on the right. Oscar felt the angel guide his steering until we were safely back on the highway. We continued our journey leaving a cloud of dust behind us, thanking the Lord for His protection. As we did so, we thought of the promise in Psalm 50:15—"Call upon me in the day of trouble: I will deliver thee, and thou shalt glorify me" (KJV). God truly heard my urgent three-word prayer that day and delivered us from a horrendous wreck. Many times we've thanked the Lord for His presence during that narrow escape from a seemingly inevitable accident.

As told by Oralee Teske.

CHAPTER 42

An Expected End

During September 2002, I flew to Venezuela with a couple of friends to work on a medical and Bible-work mission project. We worked on a project in the less populated areas of Bolivar state. One particular week, we decided to do a medical checkup in Pampatamaru, a village about an hour by plane from our base. After being cleared for takeoff, the pilot nudged our heavily loaded, little plane off the airstrip, and soon we glided through the clear sky.

From our altitude, we could see mountains surrounding us on all sides. In the distance, smaller peaks reached for the sky, but next to us, massive peaks rose like great monoliths toward the blue heavens. Below us, rivers wound their way through forested jungles and wide, open savannas. We saw waterfalls, palm trees, and little remote huts surrounded by small farm fields. As we flew over the little village where we hoped to stay for several days, we could see mud houses scattered here and there with palm leaf or metal roofing. When we landed, the natives seemed somewhat uncertain about their new visitors. Because they had no radio, as some villages do, we hadn't been able to talk to them before landing to ask if they were interested in health screening. But after landing, we asked if they would be willing to house us for a couple of nights.

We waited anxiously as our pilot spoke with the village captain in fluent Spanish. Soon we were accepted and led to the village guest house. A straight main street passed through the center of the village. On this street we saw a recently erected church in the midst of surrounding huts.

The pilot had other appointments and left us in the village. He would return for us later.

Initially the natives seemed reserved toward us. But after they realized we were there to help them, they soon warmed up. Shortly, we had our clinic set up, and physical examinations continued as the day wore on. Readily we won the villagers' confidence; everyone talked, smiled, and laughed.

As our work in the village came to a close and the long line of people visiting our makeshift clinic began to dwindle, we began packing our items in preparation to leave. It wasn't long before we heard the familiar sound of the Cessna 172 in the distance. Quickly we gathered our belongings and headed toward the airstrip. The villagers helped us load our things into the plane as we said goodbye.

Calculating the length of the runway, the elevation gain, the weight of our items, and the wind speed, our pilot determined that we would need to make two trips—one with our luggage and our nurse from Panama. The second trip would consist of Stephanie, our other volunteer nurse, and myself.

After completing the first trip, the plane returned. We were heavier this time, and we backed the plane up as far as possible to give us maximum runway space. We all hopped in and fastened our seat belts. Our pilot offered a short prayer for our safety and fired up the prop. As the plane accelerated forward, we felt the thrust of the engine pushing us firmly back into our seats.

But we were in for a surprise! About ten feet off the ground, the plane's nose dipped back down. Next, we were bouncing off the runway into a field! Suspecting that a fuel problem had developed, the pilot quickly switched to the second tank. By now we had lost speed. Stephanie and I knew something was wrong, but trusted the pilot's experience and the Lord's providence. We heard the engine catch, and slowly—ever so slowly—the plane began to climb upward into the air. Looking back to earth, we saw the open diamond-mining field we would have crashed into had the engine not started again. Comparing our movement with the ground below, I was amazed that we were still in the air. We were going very slowly. Even though it seemed strange, we continued to climb, gaining speed and altitude, little by little.

That evening, back at our base, we talked about the day's adventures. Our pilot said something I will never forget, "According to the airplane specifications, our little Cessna 172 is able to stay in the air only at a speed above forty-two knots. With a STOL kit, which we don't have, it can fly at a minimum of thirty-seven knots. We flew out of that village at thirty-five knots!"

A miracle, indeed! Truly, God sent His angels to keep our plane in the air and save us from a crash! God promises in Jeremiah 29:11, "For I know the thoughts that I think toward you, saith the LORD, thoughts of peace, and not of evil, to give you an expected end" (KJV).

As told by Ryan VanDenburgh.

CHAPTER 43

God Forgives — Let Him

As my old Buick nosed over the floating bridge, I pounded the steering wheel with my fist. "Where are You, God?" I shouted. Tears tumbled over each other and down my hot cheeks.

"I can't understand why You've forsaken us, Lord!" I continued, "I hate to leave Mother in the nursing home where help is scarce. Besides, I promised her I'd never place her in a care facility like this. She's been a good Christian all her life." I rambled on, "Now, why is she having all of these small strokes—one after another? I feel so guilty driving the 325 miles back home and leaving her here, but my husband needs me at home."

As I drove, a heavy weight of guilt crushed my head and chest. Devastated and frustrated, I felt nothing had worked out for the plan I'd had to care for my aging mother. For various reasons, keeping her in our home had lasted no longer than ten months. Caring for her in the private home of a friend didn't work out either. The nursing home proved our last resource for Mother's round-the-clock care.

Nevertheless, guilt crushed me. At the outskirts of the next little town, a sign towered like a looming giant. Its black letters caught my attention. Although I'd driven this route many times, I'd never seen that sign before sitting beside the tan church building. To this day, I'm not sure of the name of the church—Immanuel something. But the sign's bold letters burned themselves indelibly into my memory. They read, "God forgives—Let Him!"

"All right, God, You win!" I told Him. "Thank You for Your immeasurable, unmovable love, and above all for Your promise to forgive! Please make it possible for me to allow You to forgive all the blunders I've made in planning Mother's care. Somehow this guilt clings to me like a lead-laden backpack! Please help me *let* You forgive, Lord!"

As my car sped along the winding highway, I kept repeating the words on the sign. I thought about forgiveness and what it means. The best living example of forgiveness that I could recall was how my mother always forgave me so readily. I thought about the time I lost my cool and burning words toward Mother had escaped my lips. Immediately, I had seen the deep hurt on her face. I apologized. She readily and lovingly forgave me.

My thoughts rambled on to the story of the prodigal son. His father arose each new day, went to his door, and strained his eyes peering down the road for his wayward son to return. One day he couldn't believe his eyes. He saw a distant figure trudging toward home with a familiar gait. The father raced to enfold his son with loving arms of forgiveness.

"Are You really like that, God?" I asked aloud as the hot July sun dipped low and slid behind the mountains. At the same time, the load of crushing guilt also slipped from my shoulders. God's miracle of forgiveness enveloped me.

Later, at home, I read the chapter, "Faith and Acceptance," in the book *Steps to Christ*. These words spread their peace in my heart:

It is peace that you need—Heaven's forgiveness and peace and love in the soul. Money cannot buy it, intellect cannot procure it, wisdom cannot attain to it; you can never hope, by your own efforts, to secure it. But God offers it to you as a gift, "without money and without price." Isaiah 55:1. It is yours if you will but reach out your hand and grasp it. The Lord says, "Though your sins be as scarlet, they shall be as white as snow; though they be red like crimson, they shall be as wool." Isaiah 1:18. "A new heart also will I give you, and a new spirit will I put within you." Ezekiel 36:26 (p. 49).

Further along, I read, "If you believe the promise,—believe that you are forgiven and cleansed,—God supplies the fact; you are made whole" (p. 51).

During that trip, I learned a valuable lesson from a church signboard. Many times, I've thought, I'd like to thank the pastor, or whoever posted those words just for me as I wrestled with that heavy load of guilt. I've seen other words on that sign since that trip, but none jumped out to catch my attention like those words did.

It's been over a decade since this experience, and I praise God for the words on the sign and for His love and precious promises—a balm to a weary, worn, guilt-laden traveler. "God Forgives—Let Him!"

First published in Adventist Review, *July 1998.*
Used by permission.

If you enjoyed this book, you'll enjoy these as well:

An Angel's Touch
Nathalie Ladner-Bischoff. Stories of miraculous intervention and angels at work in our world today—showing that miracles still happen. Each story will make angels seem more real and build faith in God's never-ending love.
0-8163-1577-9. Paperback. US$9.99, Cdn$14.99.

In the Presence of Angels
E. Lonnie Melashenko and *Tim Crosby.* A contemporary collection of encounters with angels from Voice of Prophecy listeners.
0-8163-1261-3. Paperback. US$10.99, Cdn$16.49.

Walking With Angels
E. Lonnie Melashenko and *Brian Jones.* More true stories from the author of *In the Presence of Angels.*
0-8163-1785-2. US$12.99, Cdn$19.49.

It Must Have Been An Angel
Marjorie Lewis Lloyd. This inspiring classic contains true stories selected on the basis that the outcome has no logical explanation other than divine help.
0-8163-0363-0. Paperback. US$7.99, Cdn$11.99

Angels
Ellen G. White. Turn to any page in this precious collection of quotes to find comfort and enlightenment about the selfless love of heaven's messengers.
0-8163-1310-5. US$5.99, Cdn$8.99.

Order from your ABC by calling **1-800-765-6955**, or get online and shop our virtual store at **www.AdventistBookCenter.com.**
- Read a chapter from your favorite book
- Order online
- Sign up for email notices on new products